Studying Gaming Literacies

Gaming Ecologies and Pedagogies Series

Series Editors

Hannah R. Gerber (*Sam Houston State University, USA*)
Sandra Schamroth Abrams (*St. John's University, USA*)

Lead Editor: Hannah R. Gerber

Editorial Advisory Board

Thomas Apperley (*University of Melbourne, Australia*)
Julia Gillen (*Lancaster University, UK*)
Jayne Lammers (*University of Rochester, USA*)
Jason Lee (*The Pennsylvania State University, USA*)
Alecia Magnifico (*University of New Hampshire, USA*)
Guy Merchant (*University of Sheffield, UK*)
Michael K. Thomas (*USA*)
Mark Vicars (*Victoria University, Australia*)
Allen Webb (*Western Michigan University, USA*)
Bronwyn Williams (*University of Louisville, USA*)
Karen Wohlwend (*Indiana University, USA*)

VOLUME 3

The titles published in this series are listed at *brill.com/geps*

Studying Gaming Literacies

Theories to Inform Classroom Practice

Edited by

Antero Garcia, Shelbie Witte and Jennifer S. Dail

BRILL
SENSE

LEIDEN | BOSTON

All chapters in this book have undergone peer review.

The Library of Congress Cataloging-in-Publication Data is available online at http://catalog.loc.gov

Typeface for the Latin, Greek, and Cyrillic scripts: "Brill". See and download: brill.com/brill-typeface.

ISSN 2589-9880
ISBN 978-90-04-42982-6 (paperback)
ISBN 978-90-04-42983-3 (hardback)
ISBN 978-90-04-42984-0 (e-book)

Copyright 2020 by Koninklijke Brill NV, Leiden, The Netherlands, except where stated otherwise.
Koninklijke Brill NV incorporates the imprints Brill, Brill Hes & De Graaf, Brill Nijhoff, Brill Rodopi, Brill Sense, Hotei Publishing, mentis Verlag, Verlag Ferdinand Schöningh and Wilhelm Fink Verlag.
All rights reserved. No part of this publication may be reproduced, translated, stored in a retrieval system, or transmitted in any form or by any means, electronic, mechanical, photocopying, recording or otherwise, without prior written permission from the publisher.
Authorization to photocopy items for internal or personal use is granted by Koninklijke Brill NV provided that the appropriate fees are paid directly to The Copyright Clearance Center, 222 Rosewood Drive, Suite 910, Danvers, MA 01923, USA. Fees are subject to change.

This book is printed on acid-free paper and produced in a sustainable manner.

Contents

Foreword   VII
  Donna E. Alvermann
List of Figures   VIII
Notes on Contributors   IX

Introduction: Gaming Literacies and the Boundaries of Play   1
  Antero Garcia, Jennifer S. Dail and Shelbie Witte

PART 1
Methodological Investigations in Literacies Research

Introduction to Part 1: Methodological Investigations in Literacies Research   11
  Antero Garcia, Jennifer S. Dail and Shelbie Witte

1 Inform, Perform, Transform: Modeling In-School Youth Participatory Action Research through Gameplay   14
  Antero Garcia

2 How Youth Can Use Gaming as an Act of Creation   22
  Jennifer Wyld

3 Digital Literacy Practices for a Gaming Generation: Commercial Gaming Lessons from Adolescent Gamers   34
  Jason A. Engerman, Robert Hein, Nate Turcotte and Alison Carr-Chellman

4 Literacies of Play: Blazing the Trail, Unchartered Territories, and Hurrying Up – #TeamLaV's Interview with James Paul Gee   53
  Raúl Alberto Mora, James Paul Gee, Michael Hernandez, Sebastián Castaño, Tyrone Steven Orrego and Daniel Ramírez

PART 2
Playful Explorations

Introduction to Part 2: Playful Explorations   65
    Antero Garcia, Jennifer S. Dail and Shelbie Witte

5 Building Civic Literacy in the English Language Arts through Geospatial Play   67
    Ellen Middaugh and Jolynn A. Asato

6 Projective Worlds: Minecraft and MCAlagaësia   85
    Laura D'Aveta

7 Literacy Practice and Play: Participatory Culture in the MMORPG, *FFXIV: A Realm Reborn*   96
    Shannon R. Mortimore-Smith

Index   109

Foreword

Studying Gaming Literacies: Theories to Inform Classroom Practice packs a powerful punch. By that I mean this book charges literacy educators and educators in general to take serious notice of the impact that gaming literacies play in both young and older learners' lives. Fulfilling that charge is something else, however. For novice gamers such as myself, the learning curve can be steep. Unless, of course, a book such as this one comes along and draws us in by breaking down (and then reassembling) the various working parts of gameplay.

The editors of *Studying Gaming Literacies* know just the proper mix of research, theory, and practice. Moreover, they know authors who can write chapters about the here and now of gameplay methodologies in ways that invite other researchers and teacher educators into a discourse largely untapped in the past. Priceless artifacts (including an interview with James Paul Gee) are part and parcel of each chapter. In sum, they are the very things that open a realm of possibilities for inquiring further into a range of reading, writing, and socializing practices associated with gaming literacies.

For readers less interested in the methodological aspects of this book, there are chapters that capture both the cross-disciplinary and transdisciplinary nature of gaming literacies in relation to different subject areas, contexts, and platforms. Perhaps best of all, this book has a companion volume, *Playing with Teaching: Considerations for Implementing Gaming Literacies in the Classroom*. Developed in parallel with the research book, *Playing with Teaching* offers educators who are in close proximity to learners a compendium of instructional practices and tools for implementing the research. Taken together, the two books represent a unique blend of contemporary thinking about the relevance of gaming literacies in a world fraught with issues that require innovative strategizing and humane ways of responding.

Donna E. Alvermann
The University of Georgia
June 3, 2019

Figures

3.1   In-game text in *World of Warcraft*.   38
3.2   Assassin's Creed II.   41
6.1   Paolini's first map of Alagaësia.   91
6.2   The MCAlagaësia team's map of Alagaësia in Minecraft.   92

Notes on Contributors

Jolynn A. Asato
(PhD) is a faculty member in Teacher Education at San José State University. Her work examines culturally sustaining and social justice approaches to literacy development in a diverse and rapidly changing society.

Alison Carr-Chellman
is Dean of the College of Education, Health & Human Sciences at the University of Idaho in Moscow, and a Professor of Curriculum & Instruction there. With six books and many refereed journal articles, Dr. Carr-Chellman's focus has been on systemic change in schools, diffusion of innovations, instructional design, online learning, and boys and gaming. She conducts workshops, has a strong consulting practice across diverse contexts, and has been invited to present her work in Brazil, China, France, Norway, and New Zealand.

Sebastián Castaño
holds a B.A. in English-Spanish Education at Universidad Pontificia Bolivariana (UPB) in Medellín, Colombia. He is a researcher at the Literacies in Second Languages Project (LSLP) since 2014 and an instructor at Institución Universitaria de Envigado. His research interests include the use of English in the context of video games, with an interest in simulators, and fan fiction as a literary resource in the second language curriculum.

Jennifer S. Dail
is a Professor of English education in the Department of English at Kennesaw State University in the metro-Atlanta area of Georgia. She also directs the Kennesaw Mountain Writing Project (KMWP), a National Writing Project site serving teachers Pre-K through college in all content areas. Dail served as coeditor of SIGNAL Journal, the International Literacy Association's journal focusing on young adult literature, from 2008 to 2013. She is also an active member of several educational organizations including the National Council of Teachers of English (NCTE) and the National Writing Project (NWP). She serves on the board of the Georgia Council of Teachers of English (GCTE) as the First Vice President and Conference Director. Dail has published multiple articles on young adult literature and technology in *The ALAN Review* and has written book chapters focusing on this work as well. She also co-edited *Toward a More Visual Literacy: Shifting the Paradigm with Digital Tools and Young Adult Literature* (Rowman & Littlefield, 2018) and *Young Adult Literature and the Digital World: Textual Engagement through Visual Literacy* (Rowman & Littlefield, 2018), both with Shelbie Witte and Steven Bickmore.

Laura D'Aveta
obtained her PhD in Children's Literature at Pennsylvania State University and her MLIS at Kent State University. Her research involves readers' interactions with fantasy settings and the sense of place they develop through those interactions. Laura has taught children's literature courses, including methods and fantasy literature, at the undergraduate level in both in-residence and on-line contexts. She is currently the Humanities Librarian at Texas A&M University, where she hopes to continue her research in Children's Literature.

Jason A. Engerman
is an Assistant Professor at East Stroudsburg University within the Digital Media Technology department. His research focus is at the intersection of underrepresented populations, and their sociocultural uses of interactive digital media (such as video games) within native learning ecologies in the age of experience.

Antero Garcia
is an Assistant Professor in the Graduate School of Education at Stanford University where he studies how technology and gaming shape both youth and adult learning, literacy practices, and civic identities. Prior to completing his PhD, Antero was an English teacher at a public high school in South Central Los Angeles. His most recent research studies explore learning and literacies in tabletop roleplaying games like Dungeons & Dragons and how participatory culture shifts classroom relationships and instruction. Based on his research focused on equitable teaching and learning opportunities for urban youth through the use of participatory media and gameplay, Antero co-designed the Critical Design and Gaming School--a public high school in South Central Los Angeles. Antero's research has appeared in numerous journals including *American Educational Research Journal, Harvard Educational Review,* and *Reading Research Quarterly*. His most recent books are *Good Reception: Teens, Teachers, and Mobile Media in a Los Angeles High School* (MIT Press, 2017), *Doing Youth Participatory Action Research: Transforming Inquiry with Researchers, Educators, and Students* (Routledge, 2016, with Nicole Mirra and Ernest Morrell), and Pose, Wobble, Flow: A *Culturally Proactive Approach to Literacy Instruction* (Teachers College Press, 2015, with Cindy O'Donnell-Allen). Antero received his PhD in the Urban Schooling division of the Graduate School of Education and Information Studies at the University of California, Los Angeles.

James Paul Gee
is the Mary Lou Fulton Presidential Professor of Literacy Studies at Arizona State University and a member of the National Academy of Education. In his distinguished career spanning four decades, he has helped define fields such

as New Literacy Studies, discourse analysis, sociolinguistics, and video games research. He is the author of some of the most influential books in gaming research such as *What Video Games Have to Teach Us about Learning and Literacy* (St. Martin's Griffin, 2003, Second Edition 2007), *Situated Language and Learning* (Routledge, 2004), *Why Video Games Are Good for Your Soul* (Common Ground 2005), *Good Video Games and Good Learning: Collected Essays* (Peter Lang, 2007), and *Unified Discourse Analysis: Language, Reality, Virtual Worlds, and Video Games* (Routledge, 2014).

Robert Hein

is a former high school English teacher that is currently writing his dissertation. He is interested in researching how competitive gamers improve their skills and build communities through livestreaming platforms like *Twitch.tv*. Specifically, he wants to better understand how these "Esport" competitors are able to quickly and efficiently make the transition from novice to expert.

Michael Hernandez

is finishing his B.A. in English-Spanish Education at Universidad Pontificia Bolivariana (UPB) in Medellín, Colombia. He was a researcher at the Literacies in Second Languages Project (LSLP) between 2014 and 2019, and also working as a freelance English teacher.

Ellen Middaugh

(PhD) is a faculty member in Child and Adolescent Development at San José State University. Her work examines youth civic development, civic education and civic media literacy in the digital age.

Raúl Alberto Mora

is an Associate Professor of English Education and Literacy Studies at Universidad Pontificia Bolivariana (UPB) in Medellín, Colombia. A former school teacher and Fulbright scholar, his current research agenda, an expansion from his PhD studies in Language and Literacy at the University of Illinois, explores the emergence of English literacies across different contexts in Medellín, the use of English in the context of videogames, and the implementation of contemporary literacy paradigms in the second language curriculum, topics he studies with his research team at the Literacies in Second Languages Project (LSLP).

Shannon R. Mortimore-Smith

is an Associate Professor of English at Shippensburg University in Pennsylvania, where she teaches adolescent literature and secondary certification courses. Her interests include multimodal, 21st-century, and New Media literacy practices, including the role of comics, graphic novels, Japanese manga, and video games in the English classroom.

Tyrone Steven Orrego

is an M.A. Candidate in Education (Virtual Environment Education Emphasis) at Universidad Pontificia Bolivariana (UPB) in Medellín, Colombia. He is a student-researcher at the Literacies in Second Languages Project (LSLP) since 2014. His research interests include the use of English in the context of video games, specifically Massive Multiplayer Role-Playing Games (MMORPG), and the role of critical media literacy in the in the reconstruction of social media environments to promote critical thinking.

Daniel Ramírez

holds a B.A. in English-Spanish Education at Universidad Pontificia Bolivariana (UPB) in Medellín, Colombia. He was a researcher at the Literacies in Second Languages Project (LSLP) between 2014 and 2019, currently also working as a freelance English teacher.

Nate Turcotte

is a doctoral candidate in the Learning, Design, and Technology program at the Pennsylvania State University, in State College, Pennsylvania. His research explores teaching and learning across formal and informal technology-enhanced learning settings.

Shelbie Witte

(PhD) is the Chuck and Kim Watson Endowed Chair in Education and Professor in Adolescent Literacy and English Education at Oklahoma State University, where she directs the OSU Writing Project and the Initiative for 21st Century Literacies Research. She serves as editor (with Sara Kajder) of *Voices from the Middle*, NCTE's premiere middle-level journal. Witte has published extensively in the area of 21st Century Literacies, including *Literacy Engagement through Peritextual Analysis* (American Library Association and National Council of Teachers of English 2019) with Don Latham and Melissa Gross, *Toward a More Visual Literacy: Shifting the Paradigm with Digital Tools and Young Adult Literature* (Rowman & Littlefield, 2018) and *Young Adult Literature and the Digital World: Textual Engagement Through Visual Literacy* (Rowman & Littlefield, 2018), both with Jennifer S. Dail and Steven Bickmore.

Jennifer Wyld

received her PhD in Science Education with a focus on Free Choice Learning in 2015. Her dissertation research focused on how a Maker Education experience, particularly a computer design after-school program, impacted youth interest development for middle schoolers in an under-resourced community. Jennifer has also completed Montessori training for elementary aged children and adolescents, and taught at both of those levels in public charter and private school settings.

INTRODUCTION

Gaming Literacies and the Boundaries of Play

Antero Garcia, Jennifer S. Dail and Shelbie Witte

This book takes seriously games, their literacies, and the pedagogical possibilities of play. In so doing, this volume implicitly endorses the notion that gaming shapes powerful sociocultural contexts of learning, collaboration, and multimodal production. Whether rolling dice across a brightly rendered board or clicking and tapping a figure across a digital screen or even rollicking across a large, grassy field, gameplay is a literacy practice. Intentionally, the vast majority of games require reading and interpreting a world—virtual or physical—and making decisions within this space. This may be abstract such as in a backgammon game, but such contexts still require reading, interpreting, and decision making within these contexts.

Recognizing games as sites for learning and instruction, the chapters of this volume offer methodological contexts for exploring expansive, playful learning. In order to ground literacies scholarship on games and learning, the remainder of this introduction focuses on offering definitions to ground how we define games, play, and literacies. However, before digging into these definitions, we pause with an acknowledgement.

1 (Why) Do Games Matter?

At the time that we write this, the political landscape that shapes schooling in the U.S. and around the globe is fraught. Longstanding educational "debt" (Ladson-Billings, 2006) has meant that student achievement—based on restrictive and high stakes measures—is often divided along racial and socioeconomic lines. Interest-driven approaches to learning may be emphasized in teacher education programs today and yet schools can be seen as spaces that may not be fully engaged with the world of civic life that students are being thrust into beyond the walls of classrooms. Likewise, the teaching profession faces threats to tenure, pay compensation, and support. From the laborers within the system to the young people that demand the right to a powerful schooling experience, public education is under serious, continual threat today.

At the same time, the culture that surrounds some gaming communities has led to harassment of women, people of color, and members of the LGBTQ community. In light of these serious concerns that shape the needs and demands of schools and of supporting the learning of young people, it may feel off key to center gaming literacies research over these important issues.

However, we want to emphasize that it is precisely *because* of these contexts of fraught conditions for learning and teaching in neoliberal, western contexts that studying games and learning matter more than ever today. As powerful spaces of connected learning (Ito et al., 2013), games can harness the interests of young people and do so around topics and content not frequently focused on in schools. Likewise, games—like other texts—can be read and written critically along lines of power, authority, and resistance. From encouraging classroom engagement in virtual worlds to youth authoring liberatory identities in gaming products, games can be tools for exploration, critical production, reflection, activism. Games can reorient classrooms along new lines of power distribution, shifting authority and encouraging new types of leadership, mentoring, and empathy. And so, in grounding a common vocabulary for interpreting gaming, we want to recognize that this volume emerges to underscore gaming research working toward justice.

Additionally, as much as this is a book written about the research of games, literacy, and learning, we have worked with the authors of this book to make this a text accessible for educators, parents, and individuals curious about the possibilities of games and literacy development. As one component of these efforts, each chapter begins with key takeaways and discussion questions to encourage dialogue and personal reflection. And, though each contributor approaches this work with diverse perspectives, experiences, and ideological foundations, we center this volume around key definitions related to play, gaming, and literacy. These definitions, outlined in the next section, provide a central means for interpreting what play *means* and how it might be researched across various settings.

2   Defining the Where and What of Gaming Literacies

Games are one part of the more expansive, natural phenomenon of *play*. Not tied to solely childish—or even human—activity, play is ephemeral, often free form, and not necessarily guided by the kinds of rulesets that dictate what counts as valid, legal, *allowed* within a game. This, too, can be said of school. Formal learning can be differentiated from informal learning by spoken and unspoken rules that dictate where, how, and who participates within formal contexts like classrooms. In this sense, play can be understood as contrasted with schooling, as John Dewey (1997) noted in his framing school contexts of learning, play can be interpreted as "relief from the tedium and strain of 'regular' school work" (p. 228).

Further contextualizing this notion of play, Huizinga's (1955) foundational description of play as "a free activity standing quite consciously outside 'ordinary' life" is a key way of considering what happens within play and gaming contexts as *different* from what happens in ordinary activity (p. 13). Recognizing that play "proceeds within its own proper boundaries time and space according to fixed rules and in an orderly manner", Huizinga's framing of play as taking place within a "magic circle" offers a useful boundary of where play occurs (p. 13). These boundaries of play allow us to then make more explicit what is meant by a game happening within such a space. Specifying what counts as a game, we adopt Salen and Zimmerman's (2003) definition that "A *game* is a system in which players engage in an artificial conflict, defined by rules, that results in a quantifiable outcome" (p. 96).

This definition of a game allows us to consider analog contexts of play such as physical sports and board games as well as the complex digital ecologies of online virtual worlds. However, such a definition still means that actually *where* a game takes place can be somewhat elusive. In this we take a "layered" approach to interpreting gaming. This layered approach focuses on

> the ways that combinations of digital and nondigital practices, texts, and spaces work in concert to support meaning making; such layering is not linear in fashion, nor is it a simple or tidy accumulation of practices. Rather, it includes multidirectional and often irregular movement and interaction among and across experiences, texts, and modalities. (Abrams & Russo, 2015, p. 132)

For this volume, such a layered approach means looking at the different interactions and contexts of play. As other literacies research describes (Abrams, 2015; Garcia, 2017), the layers of gaming mean analyzing the in-game interactions in a game, the physical gestures required to enact action, the deliberation and thought required in play, and even the social and cultural worlds that mediate play and its meaning. Abrams (2017) explains that a layered approach to literacy "brings to light the intertwined, overlapping, and iterative connection among context, culture, and understanding" (p. 502). As a practical example, imagine the titular Mario of *Super Mario Bros*. The "game" of this Nintendo classic can be examined at the level of the world-weary plumber as he is maneuvered through a world of pipes and goombas and princesses needing to be saved. Too, the game can be seen as the physical gestures of fingers on a controller and the mental decisions made a player. At the same time, the social dimensions of—perhaps—playing Mario nostalgically decades after its release at a party with friends also shapes what play means and looks like. Finally, the broader world that applies meaning to Mario—and maybe offers a feminist critique that not all princesses need saving—is as important a layer to studying games as the one that minutely focused on the pixelated character with impressive jumping skills. Importantly, each of these layers are important ones for analysis and require different methodological instruments for exploration and measurement.

In describing games and learning, the notion that a game is connected to but also distinct from its metagame is an important one. We build here first on words of influential game designer, Richard Garfield (2000) who describes a metagame as "how a game interfaces outside itself" (p. 16). Taking this concept further, Gee and Hayes (2011) have adapted Gee's previous work on Discourse (1999) to differentiate the emphasis on "the software that sets up game play"—the "little g" game from the "big G game" that includes a game and its surrounding metagame. In this sense, games are a conglomeration of the products that make them work—individuals, components, rulesets, etc.—and the cultural interactions that shape them and are shaped by them.

As we look across case studies of games, literacy, and learning, these perspectives encourage readers, researchers, educators, and gamers alike to consider *where* the game is, what kinds of contexts of learning are emerging, and what affordances do these layers provide. To be clear, research on games, learning, and interactions have focused on each of these different aspects of play and each of them shape different kinds of reading, writing, and production practices. The literacies of play are many.

For this volume, we combine these layered perspectives of play with the recognition that they are encompassed by a broader metagame. In this sense, gaming literacies—the exploration of reading, writing, and productive social practices in gaming contexts—include cultural exploration, the affinity spaces of players, individual meaning making, the affordances of gaming platforms (e.g. gaming consoles and tabletop boards), and the specific virtual worlds in which games are enacted (Garcia, 2017). This definition both embraces the broad definition (and layers) of gaming as well as an expansive notion that there are multiple literacies, following the tradition of sociocultural research informed by the new literacies studies (e.g. Street 1994). This framing of literacies considers "new types" of literacy "especially digital literacies and literacy practices embedded in popular culture" (Gee, 2010, p. 31).

3   Studying Intersections of Play and Literacy

Like any domain in which individuals learn, mentor, and apprentice, gaming spaces are rife with formal and informal learning opportunities. They are deeply rooted in the interactions of players with systems and with one another. As such the same tools for exploring learning and teaching may often be employed in unpacking gaming literacies at the table. To this end, we recognize that a large portion of the methodological tools for studying digital and non-digital games echo those used by educational research broadly. That being said, the possibilities for studying within game-based virtual worlds continue to grow for researchers (e.g. Boellstorff, Nardi, Pearce, & Taylor, 2012; Hine, 2011; Pearce, & Artemesia, 2009). Likewise, when considering digital games, advances in digital methodologies are also substantially shifting how meaning is constructed in these environments (cf. Gerber, Abrams, Curwood, & Magnifico, 2016).

Finally, in both digital and analog settings, the role of materiality, temporality, and space are profound and often underexplored. Where games take place, what materials shape them, and across what kinds of temporal boundaries are important indicators of how games progress and what kinds of interactions occur within them. Such topics of inquiry focus the research possibilities of gaming on the intersections of materials, players, and outcomes. These are literacy-driven topics; in their most basic form, these questions can be distilled to three simple considerations: what is written? by whom? and what does it mean?

Of course, these questions grow complicated in even the most mundane of gaming settings, and the chapters in this volume highlight the possibilities of literacy-focused research in gaming settings. That being said, engaging in these research practices still requires the scrutiny and ethical standards that we adhere to across research domains. Even within gaming settings, settler-colonial practices mean that research can stifle, harm, and silence values, identities, and perspectives. To this extent, we encourage gaming researchers to heed the words of Toni Morrison (1997): "We die. That may be the meaning of life. But we do language. That may be the measure of our lives". Building meaning, interpreting language, exploring affordances of *fun* are serious endeavors. The complex and symbolic systems of learning at the heart of play must be explored humanely. Playing with research and researching play are dialectical practices that require methodological rigor.

4   Looking Ahead

The chapters that follow are organized into two parts. The first, "Methodological Investigation in Literacies Research", represents studies that highlight *how* literacies research within and using games may be conducted. These chapters are case-based and demonstrate a variety of qualitative approaches to literacies research with games and learning. This section also includes Mora et al.'s interview with James Paul Gee. A recognized leader in literacies research, games, and learning, Gee's words here reflect on both the past research shaping the foundations of this book as well as on where advances in gaming research methodology and learning are headed.

The second part of this book emphasizes three different contexts of play-based research. Like the first half of this book, these chapters illustrate play within physical environments, in online virtual worlds, and in collaborative settings of young people working across classrooms and virtual worlds. We see these chapters emphasizing the methodological perspectives raised in the first part of the book and highlight the different spaces and *layers* of gaming that can be studied and explored.

We conclude this Introduction with a call for playful practices in research. Though the scope of gaming and literacies research is focused on individuals exploring, learning, and interacting in game-like settings, the research we uphold as an academic community continues to build from the sterile auspices of positivist research traditions; we call for playful research that sustains the same feelings of delight, surprise, and elucidation possible when engaged in the flow-like settings of gaming environments.

Finally, we should note that this book was developed in conjunction with a sister text, *Playing in the Classroom: Games, Literacies, and Youth Culture in the 21st Century*. This companion volume focuses on pedagogical approaches to games and literacies. The research foundations in this volume provide deeper context for interpreting the teaching practices in the other volume and—conversely—that volume provides further instructional considerations for the research shared here. Collectively these two volumes present an ongoing praxis-driven conversation about the states of play and literacy in contemporary learning. The boundaries of research and teaching and of playing and learning are often non-existent and we recognize a productive bleeding of the approaches and intellectual contributions across both volumes.

References

Abrams, S. S. (2015). *Integrating virtual and traditional learning in 6–12 classrooms: A layered literacies approach to multimodal meaning making*. New York, NY: Routledge.

Abrams, S. S. (2017). Emotionally crafted experiences: Layering literacies in minecraft. *The Reading Teacher, 70*(4), 501–506.

Abrams, S. S., & Russo, M. P. (2015). Layering literacies and contemporary learning. *Journal of Adolescent & Adult Literacy, 59*(2), 131–135.

Boellstorff, T., Nardi, B., Pearce, C., & Taylor, T. L. (2012). *Ethnography and virtual worlds: A handbook of method.* Princeton, NJ: Princeton University Press.

Dewey, J. (1997). *Democracy and education: An introduction to the philosophy of education.* New York, NY: Free Press.

Garcia, A. (2017). Space, time, and production: Games and the new frontier of digital literacies. In K. A. Mills, A. Stornaiuolo, A. Smith, & J. Z. Pandya (Eds.), *Handbook of writing, literacies, and education in digital cultures* (pp. 198–209). New York, NY: Routledge.

Garfield, R. (2000). Metagames. In J. Dietz (Ed.), *Horsemen of the apocalypse: Essays on roleplaying* (pp. 14–21). Charleston, IL: Jolly Rogers Games.

Gee, J. P. (2010). *New digital media and learning as an emerging area and "worked examples" as one way forward.* Cambridge, MA: MIT Press.

Gee, J. P., & Hayes, E. R. (2012). *Language and learning in the digital age.* New York, NY: Routledge.

Gerber, H. R., Abrams, S. S., Curwood, J. S., & Magnifico, A. M. (2016). *Conducting qualitative research of learning in online spaces.* Thousand Oaks, CA: Sage Publications.

Hine, C. (2011). *Virtual ethnography.* New York, NY: Sage Publications.

Huizinga, J. (1955). *Homo ludens: A study of the play-element in culture.* Boston, MA: The Beacon Press.

Ito, M., Gutiérrez, K., Livingstone, S., Penuel, B., Rhodes, J., Salen, K., ... Watkins, C. J. (2013). *Connected learning: An agenda for research and design.* Irvine, CA: Digital Media and Learning Research Hub.

Ladson-Billings, G. (2006). From the achievement gap to the education debt: Understanding achievement in U.S. schools. *Educational Researcher, 35*(7), 3–12.

Morrison, T. (1997). *Lecture and speech of acceptance, upon the award of the Nobel prize for literature, delivered in Stockholm on the seventh of December, nineteen hundred and ninety-three.* New York, NY: A.A. Knopf.

Pearce, C., & Artemesia. (2009). *Communities of play: Emergent cultures in multiplayer games and virtual worlds.* Cambridge, MA: MIT Press.

Salen, K., & Zimmerman, E. (2004). *Rules of play: Game design fundamentals.* Cambridge, MA: MIT Press.

Street, B. (1994). What's "new" in new literacy studies? Critical approaches to literacy in theory and practice. *Current Issues in Comparative Education, 5*(2), 77–91.

PART 1

Methodological Investigations in Literacies Research

Introduction to Part 1: Methodological Investigations in Literacies Research

Antero Garcia, Jennifer S. Dail and Shelbie Witte

The four chapters in this part begin a conversation about *how* literacies research within and around games can be conducted. Recognizing the myriad contexts from which gaming research stems, the tensions that exist within these cultures and within the academic fields studying them, and the various methodological approaches that have been undertaken in digital and analog contexts of play (e.g. Fernández-Vara, 2015; Montola, Stenros, & Wærn, 2009; Zagal & Deterding, 2018), this part intentionally offers playful breadcrumbs for engaging in and understanding literacies research in gaming settings. To be clear, these chapter do not speak as definitive "how to" guides for the innovative gaming and literacies research to come. Instead, we see these chapters as sparking conversation and engaging in several central tenets to consider in moving research further into the worlds of play, learning, and literacy. And we hope you build on the questions offered in each chapter as guideposts for sustaining your own research practices within games and literacies.

As a section, these chapters point to the broad methodological and analytic scope of gaming literacies research. There are ample opportunities for play, for learning, and for empirical understanding of the spaces and communities involved in these activities. As a result, we encourage your reading of this section to consider how the different methodological approaches these authors take up prod at their problems of practice differently.

For example, one such tension is *where* such literacies research takes place and with whom. Garcia's chapter considers the positionality of literacies research—designing a context of youth participatory action research (Garcia, 2017; Mirra, Garcia, & Morrell, 2016) in which young people playfully research and seek to instantiate change *through* gaming. Focusing on classroom-based contexts of analog play, this chapter pushes on who gets to do research and what kinds of tensions exist within this negotiation.

Similarly, Wyld's chapter, looks at the possibilities and limitations of after school contexts of learning for young people. The flexibilities of space, materials, and adult relationships highlight the contexts of interaction in one study. Likewise, Engerman, Hein, Turcotte, and Carr-Chellman chapter explores forms of play across four years and several different kinds of games. Importantly, the differences in literacy affordances, learning opportunities, and modes of engagement are highlighted as these researchers look closely *across* these spaces and platforms of participation.

Importantly, Engerman et al.'s chapter also highlights a very different kind of "where" when considering gaming literacies research. Emphasizing the role of gender, of videogames as a medium frequently targeted for their questionable content, and of health-related concerns raised in popular media, this chapter considers the sociopolitical location of games and—in turn—literacies research within and around videogames. Considering the "toxic meritocracy" (Paul, 2018) that surrounds videogame culture, this chapter brings out a necessary dimension of literacies research design.

Finally, we conclude this section with Mora et al.'s interview with James Gee. As a member of the New London Group, a leader within games, learning, and literacies, and a constantly curious writer and researcher, Gee offers both a historical perspective on a nascent field and a reflection on the tensions that exist in collaboratively field-building around a medium and cultural practice often associated with young people.

Methodologically and analytically, these chapters highlight several starting points literacies researchers might take and expand upon today. Engerman et al.'s chapter, for example, is grounded in the cultural-historical traditions that center how meaning is mediated and jointly constructed (e.g. Gallego, Cole, & Laboratory of Comparative Human Cognition, 2001; Pacheco & Gutiérrez, 2009) by participants within complex learning ecologies. Wyld's grounding in models of connected learning and Ito's (2010) framing of young people "hanging out, messing around, and geeking out", centers the shifting interests and literacy practices of youth that are regularly engaged in digital practices, cultures, and communities. In contrast, Garcia's chapter focuses on games *as* research methodology, recruiting and working alongside young people playfully for processes of transformation.

We curated these chapters hoping to offer a snapshot of *some* ways literacy research is undertaken within and with games. Knowing new literacy practices may demand new modes of inquiry, the epistemological and ontological assumptions that undergird gaming research contexts are continually re-analyzed. These chapters serve as an invitation for you to partake in such an epic—and potentially gameful—quest.

References

Fernández-Vara, C. (2015). *Introduction to game analysis*. New York, NY: Routledge.

Gallego, M. A., Cole, M., & Laboratory of Comparative Human Cognition. (2001). Classroom culture and culture in the classroom. In V. Richardson (Ed.), *Handbook of research on teaching* (4th ed., pp. 951–997). Washington, DC: American Educational Research Association.

Garcia, A. (2017). *Good reception: Teens, teachers, and mobile media in a Los Angeles high school.* Cambridge, MA: MIT Press.

Ito, M. (Ed.). (2010). *Hanging out, messing around, and geeking out: kids living and learning with new media.* Cambridge, MA: MIT Press.

Mirra, N., Garcia, A., & Morrell, E. (2016). *Doing youth participatory action research: Transforming inquiry with researchers, educators, and students.* New York, NY: Routledge.

Montola, M., Stenros, J., & Wærn, A. (2009). *Pervasive games: Theory and design.* Amsterdam & Boston, MA: Elsevier/Morgan Kaufmann.

Pacheco, M., & Gutiérrez, K. (2008). Cultural-historical approaches to literacy, teaching and learning. In C. Compton-Lilly (Ed.), *Breaking the silence: Recognizing the social and cultural resources students bring to the classroom* (pp. 60–77). Newark, DE: International Reading Association.

Paul, C. A. (2018). *The toxic meritocracy of video games: Why gaming culture is the worst.* Minneapolis, MN: University of Minnesota Press.

Zagal, J. P., & Deterding, S. (2018). *Role-playing game studies: Transmedia foundations.* New York, NY: Routledge.

CHAPTER 1

Inform, Perform, Transform: Modeling In-School Youth Participatory Action Research through Gameplay

Antero Garcia

1   Overarching Questions

1. In designing for learning and research *alongside* youth, in what ways could you adapt a model like Inform, Perform, Transform for a specific context?
2. What *stories* do games present for youth and educators to explore? Who authors these stories and in what modalities?
3. How do technologies shape the modes of play? What literacy practices do they afford?

2   Introduction

In the spring of 2011 the 17 ninth-grade students in my period-three class began receiving cryptic messages from a guileless spider. Using a class set of iPod Touches, the students dialogued with this mysterious talking animal and came up with a series of questions about their school and local community, including, "Why is there an absence of love in South Central Los Angeles?" and "What perpetuates stereotypes in South Central?" and others. Through research and conversation, students were provoked by their eight-legged confidant to subvert traditional stereotypes about their school space and to rewrite the school space around them.

Through the fictional premise of gameplay, these students blurred the line between research and role-play as part of my class curriculum, and—in doing so—helped me explore the structural challenges of enacting youth participatory action research (YPAR) within the context of a formal classroom space. As an experienced high school teacher and as a researcher, I was interested in the ways student ownership of critical research through YPAR could be motivated through principles of gaming. As a result, I created Ask Anansi, an alternate reality game (ARG) played in the "real world" by weaving elements of storytelling and fiction into the environment played as part of the class experience (Garcia & Niemeyer, 2017). The game drove the research process in my classroom and provided the students with a structure for their work. While I detail the co-developed research model of this game in the rest of this chapter, the full game's design document and related materials can be found in *Good Reception: Teens, Teachers, and Mobile Media in a Los Angeles High School* (Garcia, 2017).

3. School Context

The high school this activity took place in is one of the oldest public high schools in the city of Los Angeles. With a student population of approximately 3,400 during the year of this game, it was one of the largest in the city. Its demographics mirrored those of its surrounding community: 83% Latino, 15% African American, and 2% multiracial with an English Language Learner group that made up 39% of the student population. Eighty-seven percent of the students received free or reduced-price lunch (California Dept. of Ed. 2010). Only 35% of students graduated and the majority of these students did not graduate eligible to enroll in most four-year universities (UCLA IDEA 2010). In a deliberate effort to erase a cultural past of uprising, resistance, and negative press through renaming the community, mainstream media and the governing agencies of Los Angeles now refer to the community as "South Los Angeles." However, despite the flooding of "South Los Angeles" messaging in media, I never heard any of my students refer to this community as anything but "South Central."

4. Playing with YPAR

My work with students in this project is guided by three principles of Participatory Action Research as delineated by Alice McIntyre (2000, p. 128):
1. The collective investigation of a problem.
2. The reliance on indigenous knowledge to better understand that problem.
3. The desire to take individual and/or collective action to deal with the stated problem.

McIntyre saw the research process as "engaging in processes that position youth as agents of inquiry and 'experts' about their own lives" (2000, p. 126). Though documented examples of YPAR have occurred in extracurricular spaces (Morrell, 2008; Romero et al., 2008; Stovall et al., 2009), I wanted to know how to support YPAR within the traditional 8:00 a.m. to 3:00 p.m. hours of the school day. For me, instilling youth-driven research within the classroom is about shifting to a "new culture of learning" (Thomas & Brown, 2011) and, in particular, opening up space to foster the interests and knowledge of my students. I attempted to do this through sustained gameplay for seven weeks.

Not an app or a board game, Ask Anansi is a game that students experience through role-playing, researching, and imagining over the course of seven weeks. This gaming experience guided students toward a process of identifying specific topics for critical inquiry and playing through the act of engagement and participation.

In *Homo Ludens: A Study of the Play-Element in Culture*, Johan Huizinga described the space in which games are played as a "magic circle," emphasizing that the main characteristic of play is "that it is free;" furthermore, "[p]lay is not 'ordinary' or 'real' life. It is rather a stepping out of 'real' life into a temporary sphere of activity" (1949, p. 8). The magic circle of gameplay is one in which role-playing, acting, and behavior exceed social norms; it is here that students can comfortably pose, flex, and experiment in ways they may not typically be expected to participate or behave. Casting this magic circle around the activities in my classroom and shielding our inquiry from pressure for students' social conformity, I created Ask Anansi as an ARG that steeps student action and problem-posing in a tradition of West African folklore.

In Ask Anansi student participation is community-centered; students engage in inquiry-based problem solving by communicating with Anansi and helping to unravel the stories he tells. The trickster spider-god of Caribbean folklore, Anansi, has answers and solutions to any question students can imagine. Students pose research questions to Anansi. Sample questions that students asked in the class included a focus on the perpetuation of stereotypes in South Central and the "absence of love" within the school's community. Anansi's responses to such questions, however, are not always the most clear; he likes tricks, riddles, and befuddlement. As a result, student interaction with the fictitious character led them to document, interview, and collect evidence related to their research questions; communicating with Anansi acts as an engine to drive YPAR research, revision, and theory building. The Ask Anansi gaming environment allowed students to act, question, and engage in simultaneously critical and playful inquiry.

Over several days, I facilitated class-wide discussion where students shared images, individual research, and reflections they made about the school and neighborhood space in which they live. Through these discussions the students and I noticed prominent themes in the frustrations students had and concerns they shared about their community. From these patterns, students formed the research questions stated at the beginning of this article, and I attempted to move the class inquiry beyond the walls of the classroom. Exploring the campus for spaces that reflected student research topics, we participated in a whole-class scavenger hunt; students wrote clues that guided players to spaces on and around the school related to topics of equity and power. These clues led students to student-created QR code badges hidden at SCHS; encoded were questions to stimulate participants' reflections on the space and its usage within the school. To fit within the theme of the alternate-reality game, the scavenger-hunt reward badges were wrapped scroll-like inside the ring portion of black plastic spider rings, the type typically given out to children around Halloween.

As an example, I wrote a clue titled "The Hidden Vestibule" to demonstrate the writing and searching process for students:

> To find my last badge, you need to follow the origins of your curricular materials. From where does the ocean of learning materials flow? Can you find the origin? Once you arrive, you may have to do some climbing.

The clue led to an abandoned classroom space in an upstairs alcove of the school's textbook room. Students were signaled that they were in the right location by a solitary spider dangling from a string in the doorway of the run-down room.

After this brief demonstration, students spent a week busily creating and revising clues that I prepared to distribute to their peers. Students chose their locations and clues based on the research they had conducted. By that Friday, each student had received a sizeable workbook of more than eighty original clues. With a class period and a weekend to search on their own, students hunched over clues and copies of campus maps. During the class period students were encouraged to develop strategies to find as many clues as possible, and they scanned their maps plotting not only how to retrieve clues based on where they speculated the clues were hidden, but also how to do so efficiently. Two students, Elizabeth and Marjane, each grouped clues by proximity to each other in an effort to find badges (with QR codes) that were closest to one another and build a mapped journey of searching across the campus. Elizabeth started by searching for several locations in our building before venturing to the outside quad, the neighboring building, and the main lunch area, and two badges were located near the school's auditorium.

In the final step of the game students were asked to write very short descriptions of what they encountered along with an informative or intriguing title.

The assignment also asked the students to conclude each of their descriptions by posing a question to the individuals that read them.

After these cards were written and then revised by a classmate, students posted the cards prominently in the spaces where they had originally hidden clues. The hidden badges morphed into prominent public displays of knowledge and dialogue. One of Minerva's clues, once hidden underneath the dusty water fountain outside our classroom, for instance, was later translated by her into a notecard that was taped directly above the water fountain, unavoidably within the line of sight of anyone using the fountain. Though water fountains may seem like minor features of a school campus, the students' publicly voiced disdain for the fountain's condition demonstrates a resistance to the traditional power structures within the school.

5 Inform, Perform, Transform

This brief description of the scavenger hunt sequence of Ask Anansi illustrates the ways youth can recontextualize their physical surroundings through game-based YPAR. This sequence followed a key thematic approach to critical transformative practice: Inform, Perform, Transform. This approach was adapted from my own experiences with another alternate-reality game, the Black Cloud (Niemeyer, Garcia, & Naima, 2009), in which students' actions focused on improving local air quality and were informed by data collected at various nearby locations. As its name states, this approach has three thematic components used within the classroom, and each of these has distinct activities tied to it.

5.1 *Inform*

During the "Inform" phase students gather, analyze, and collate information to produce their own, original work. Students furthered their acquisition of three types of knowledge during the "Inform" phase of the unit described here:
– Local, tacit expertise of their communities (recognizing, too, that "communities" are fluid and contested spaces e.g. Philip et al., 2013).
– Conceptual understanding of the function of gameplay and problem-posing inquiry.
– Functional literacy skills including writing challenging, engaging clues, and properly logging and reflecting on found items; these skills were primarily developed through student use of their mobile media devices to collect, analyze, and share research data while the students were not tethered to the desks and seats of a classroom.

5.2 Perform

Within the "Perform" component students use the knowledge and information acquired through their informational inquiries, and produce/perform new work that is tied to a larger critical, conceptual, and/or academic goal.

In this unit students developed scavenger hunt clues for their classmates, hid them in and around their school space, and then later searched for classmates' clues.

5.3 Transform

In the "Transform" component students extend their performance toward publicly shared knowledge and action, and focus on directly impacting and critically transforming their world.

Students adapted the closed, class-only scavenger hunt into a curated public exhibit to impact the public's reading and interpretation of the South Central community.

This process allowed students to share their own body of knowledge, while the teacher acted as facilitator in this process and encouraged transformative performative action.

6 Conclusion: Assessing In-School Participatory Action Research

As I continued to develop and guide students throughout the gameplay of Ask Anansi, students expressed to me the ways this activity felt "different" from what they had done in other classes. While I felt enthusiastic about the student responses and what they may mean for in-school YPAR, I also realized that a significant challenge also loomed in extending this work in sustainable ways. The challenge with this project was not one of motivation or of finding the "right" question for students to investigate and then later act upon. My challenge related to creating democratic decision making and planning within the formal confines of a classroom.

While my classroom practice subscribed to critical pedagogical efforts of distributing knowledge and moving toward world-facing stances of engagement with curriculum (Duncan-Andrade & Morrell, 2008; Freire, 1970), this classroom is one that is still legally bound to teacher-authority and to pre-existing socio-cultural assumptions from students about classroom spaces; students and school administrators have specific understandings of what schooling looks and feels like.

Although a "new culture of learning" that Douglas Thomas and John Seely Brown (2011) illustrated as being a result of participatory media and culture can signal ripe possibilities for learning, students and teachers alike are entrenched in an entirely different paradigm. The shift from one culture of learning to another is not a simple transition. As mandated sources of authority, forms of standardized testing, and teacher evaluations based on these tests drive "schooling" today, a pedagogy of "thinking about people as researchers, as agents of change, as constructors of knowledge, actively involved in the dialectical process of action and reflection aimed at individual and collective change" feels difficult to implement (McIntyre, 2000, pp. 148–49).

With Ask Anansi I ultimately relied on the fictitious Anansi to liberate the classroom space and help weave webs for developing the critical agents within my classroom. I intended for the lessons we wove in my class to continue to be drawn upon and developed long after my students graduates from SCHS. I intended for the lessons to help weave powerful civic lessons for the future of South Central.

Acknowledgement

This chapter was originally published as Garcia, A. (2012). Inform, perform, transform: Modeling in-school youth participatory action research through gameplay. *Knowledge Quest, 41*(1), 46–50. It is adapted and reprinted here with permission from the American Library Association.

References

California Department of Education. (2010). *DataQuest*. Retrieved from http://dq.cde.ca.gov/Dataquest

Duncan-Andrade, J., & Morrell, E. (2008). *The art of critical pedagogy: Possibilities for moving from theory to practice in urban schools*. New York, NY: Peter Lang.

Freire, P. (1970). *Pedagogy of the oppressed*. New York, NY: Herder and Herder.

Garcia, A. (2017). *Good reception: Teens, teachers, and mobile media in a Los Angeles high school*. Cambridge, MA: MIT Press.

Garcia, A., & Niemeyer, G. (Eds.). (2017). *Virtual, visible, and viable: Alternate reality games and the cusp of digital gameplay*. New York, NY: Bloomsbury.

Huizinga, J. (1949). *Homo ludens: A study of the play-element in culture*. London: Routledge.

McIntyre, A. (2000). Constructing meaning about violence, school, and community: Participatory action research with urban youth. *Urban Review, 32*(2), 123–54.

Morrell, E. (2008). Six summers of YPAR: Learning, action, and change in urban education. In J. Cammarota & M. Fine (Eds.), *Revolutionizing education: Youth participatory action research in motion* (pp. 155–184). New York, NY: Routledge.

Niemeyer, G., Garcia, A., & Naima, R. (2009). *Black cloud: Patterns towards da future* (pp. 1073–1082). MM '09: Proceedings of the 17th ACM International Conference on Multimedia, Association for Computing Machinery, New York, NY.

Philip, T. M., Way, W., Garcia, A., Schuler-Brown, S., & Navarro, O. (2013). When educators attempt to make "community" a part of classroom learning: The dangers of (mis)appropriating students' communities into schools. *Teaching and Teacher Education, 34*, 174–183.

Romero, A., et al. (2008). 'The opportunity if not the right to see': The social justice education project. In J. Cammarota & M. Fine (Eds.), *Revolutionizing education: Youth participatory action research in motion* (pp. 131–151). New York, NY: Routledge.

Stovall, D., Calderon, A., Carrera, L., & King, S. (2009). Youth, media, and justice: Lessons from the Chicago doc your bloc project. *Radical Teacher, 86*, 50–58.

Thomas, D., & Brown, J. S. (2011). *A new culture of learning: Cultivating the imagination for a world of constant change*. Lexington, KY: CreateSpace.

UCLA Institute for Democracy, Education, and Access. (2010). *California educational opportunity report*. UC Regents. Retrieved from
http://idea.gseis.ucla.edu/publications/eor-10/eor-2010-ed-op-in-hard-times

CHAPTER 2

How Youth Can Use Gaming as an Act of Creation

Jennifer Wyld

1   Overarching Questions

1. What are some example of "authentic tools" in your setting?
2. What are some of the different identities you see others enact?
3. What are settings in which you engage in different levels of participation? How do the different levels reflect your experience with these activities?
4. How does technology enable access for those who are enacting "geeking out"? What are advantages and disadvantages of this?

1   Introduction

Research has identified adolescence as a critical age group in relationship to interest development. During the time period between middle childhood and adolescence, there are shifts in interest that have consequences for the pursuit of further education and even careers (Tai, Liu, Maltese, & Fan, 2006). Interest is an important factor for learning, motivation, and attention (Hidi & Renninger, 2006). Although schooling is a leading activity for adolescents, it is not the primary activity where interests develop. The activities engaged in outside of and beyond the school day can play a big role in what interests are developed (Falk & Dierking, 2010). Free Choice Learning is a field that explores learning experiences outside of formal classroom settings, such as museums, libraries, aquariums, etc. (Azevedo, 2011; Falk, 2001; Falk & Dierking, 2010, 2011). A relatively new player in the Free-Choice Learning (FCL) arena, the Maker movement, offers learners interest-driven, experiential, often collaborative, and process-oriented activities ranging from game design (computer-based, card, or table top games) and robotics, to sewing LEDS into clothing. Learners can engage in Maker activities at home, in an FCL setting, as part of the school day or extended school day, or in community settings. Maker educational experiences offer opportunities for individuals to come together and explore their interests in settings that encourage collaboration and the sharing of resources, ideas, authentic skills, and tools.

Free Choice Learning considers learning as a situated experience, with personal, physical, and socio-cultural contexts (Falk & Dierking, 2000, 2011). The analysis of the three interrelated contexts, the Personal, Physical, and Socio-cultural context qualities of a new media Maker setting is critical to understanding whether, and if so, how such spaces can be used to support the interest and identity work undertaken by youth around STEM. This study specifically explores this work around technology and offers insights to help address the lack of adolescent engagement in conventional STEM learning experiences, particularly among youth from under-resourced communities and underrepresented groups. Such findings have the potential to contribute to the lack of diversity among youth choosing to study post-secondary STEM, workers in STEM careers and youth and adults engaged in STEM leisure pursuits and avocations. In addition, findings may offer ideas for how to design other alternative learning settings.

2 Methodology

I conducted a mixed-methods study with early adolescents from an under-represented community, who all participated in an intensive, nine-week after school game design program, Pixel Arts Game Design. Ito et al.'s (2013) genres of participation provided an analytical frame for assessing the Maker experience. These genres are explained later in this chapter. I leveraged a variety of quantitative and qualitative tools to offer a rich view of this Maker experience. Research methods included observations of the activities, interactions, and conversations in which the youth engaged each week of the club. I also used the tool Personal Meaning Mapping (circa 2013) to gather information on the youths' identities around technology as a pre-/post-artifact. I conducted in-depth interviews at the start and conclusion of the experience. In analyzing the interviews, artifacts, and observations, I focused on both behaviors and pronoun usage as a marker of identity shift. Findings showed that the new media Maker space afforded diverse and underserved youth in the study new ways to identify with technology, explore their interests, and re-Make their identities with each other, near peer mentors, and adult facilitators.

3 Statement of the Problem

Identity is a fluid construct that develops throughout life. The roles offered to members of a culture may limit the possible selves of individuals due to many factors including: age, sex, gender, and social status. Despite this, individuals can change and make choices about who and how they want to be. The interests an individual has and explores can also impact their identity (Renninger, 2009), which includes both the self-image and the images held by others as a result of those interests.

Previous research (Azevedo, 2011; Tai et al., 2006), shows that children who have an interest in their chosen subject are more likely to be motivated learners. They are also more likely to seek out challenging and difficult tasks, use effective learning strategies, make optimal use of feedback, and even consider learning to be fun. This is true for all topics individuals feel passionate about (Thomas & Seely Brown, 2011). Furthermore, youth who are able to develop and sustain their interest are more likely to become adults who identify with these topics, pursue these interests informally and at work, and make informed decisions (Renninger & Hidi, 2002).

Education and museum learning researchers have conducted studies to understand how individuals learn in specific settings (Falk & Dierking, 2011). There is an assumption that people learn more effectively and put more effort into learning about topics in which they are personally interested. One of the relevant axioms in the field is, if an interest is to develop from a situational interest to an individual interest, that interest must be explored and developed in multiple settings (Hidi & Renninger, 2006). Although this process is not well understood, some researchers have started to articulate ideas of life-long, life-wide and life-deep learning (Falk & Dierking, 2011; Thomas & Seely Brown, 2011).

4 Theoretical Framework and Review of the Relevant Literature

Thinkers in the field are finding ways to combine levels of interest development with levels of participation. They are weaving together the four phases of identity development of Hidi and Renninger with Ito et al.'s work on genres of participation. Hidi and Renniger developed a four-phase model of interest development (2006) that posits that interest is first extrinsically triggered by a situation, but, if maintained, can develop into an individual interest that tends to be more intrinsically motivated. The four phases in this model are: triggered situational interest, maintained situational interest, individual interest, and well-developed individual interest. Ito et al. (2013) focused on the social and active qualities of individual engagement with media, what they were doing with media, and who they were doing it with. The focus on participation, as opposed to consumption or internalization, presupposes an active role for the youth. From their research on youth interacting with new media, Ito et al. recognize different genres of participation. One level of analysis looks at whether participation is friendship-driven or interest-driven. While friendship-driven participation may lead to interest-driven participation, a new social group often arises, which is based on the similar interests rather than proximity or past shared experiences. Within interest-driven participation, there is a trajectory from "hanging out" to "messing around", to "geeking out", that youth may progress along, as their interest and participation deepens (Ito et al., 2013). The focus is on the different modes of participation rather than categories of individuals, as youth may exhibit different levels of participation in different contexts (Horst, Herr-Stephenson, & Robinson, 2013; Ito et al., 2013).

As identity shifts across time and setting, so does behavior. At the level of "hanging out" the focus is on maintaining social relationships with peers using new media, such as the internet and social media sites. The on-line, networked experiences youth engage in supplement physical interactions, allowing them to connect across barriers of place and time. This level of participation is largely friendship-driven (Horst et al., 2013). It has also been described as how an individual "learns to be" in a setting, where the work of creating a social identity takes place (Thomas & Seely Brown, 2011).

A more intense level of participation is described as "messing around" which encompasses activities such as using the internet to find more information on topics or skills, using trial and error to figure out how things work within a specific medium, and learning how to find and use resources available to them in regards to new media interests. When "messing around" youth are engaged in self-directed learning. They seek out and practice skills with the new media on their own (Ito et al., 2013). As the individual moves beyond the more social nature of the context, they focus on the content and skills of the setting. This is the point where knowing and making meet (Thomas & Seely Brown, 2011). There is a shift from social agency work at the "hanging out" genre, to the development of personal agency, as mastery of the tools/media is the focus.

Lastly, there is the genre of "geeking out". As implied by the popular cultural understanding of a "geek", individuals demonstrating this level of participation exhibit a greater level of intensity around their engagement and commitment to a topic or tool. This is usually accompanied by specialized knowledge and frequent participation (Horst et al., 2013). At this level, there is also typically participation in a community of similarly "geeky" individuals, and the social relationships have expanded beyond peers one would meet in their physical daily settings, to include a more diverse group, as in an on-line environment. At this phase, location and age are less important factors in building social networks (Horst et al., 2013; Ito et al., 2013). Individuals are able to access and leverage both social and technical resources with skills and connections created while "hanging out" and "messing around" (Thomas & Seely Brown, 2011). When "geeking out", individuals engage in learning that is "intense, autonomous, and interest-driven" (Ito et al., 2013; Thomas & Seely Brown, 2011).

In their work through the Stanford FabLab, Worsley and Blikstein combine both levels of situational interest (both triggered and maintained) to match up with "hanging out". Individual interest fits with "messing around, as interest strengthens, so does commitment to the activity or project. Lastly, a well-developed interest is exhibited by the level of "geeking out, where the individual follows up on their interest in a variety of settings, using a variety of resources, social and material, to often work independently, or with a small group of individuals—either virtually or physically, who share a similar level of interest and expertise" (Worsley & Blikstein, 2013). The challenge for FabLabs and Maker Spaces is to create entry points and support for individuals at all of these different stages and levels of interest and engagement.

The media available to youth in a culture provide outlets for creative expression and social action (Ito et al., 2013). While media, such as television, music, or books, have long been a part of popular culture, new media refer to the recent development of interactive, networked gaming and social communication sites. These media necessitate active social engagement by their nature. The term "new" is used by researchers to denote more than any one specific media platform, aiming to capture what is new at this moment in a situational, relational, and universal context (Ito et al., 2013). This media is constantly changing, with updates, newer versions, and even platforms replacing each other in popularity. For example, some research conducted in the earlier part of this decade discussed Myspace, a social networking platform that has subsequently been largely replaced by Facebook in popularity.

New media are associated with youth culture, agency, and voice (Ito et al., 2013). These include social network sites, media fandoms, and networked gaming sites. While adults populate sites like Facebook, Linked In, Match.com, Twitter, and blogs, youth are frequenting Facebook, YouTube, Instagram, Snapchat, LiveJournal, Tumblr, and online gaming (personal youth interviews, 2015). By and large, these are sites used to create content, often fan culture based on elements such as characters from books, movies, or television, and to connect with peers socially. Even sites used by both adults and youth evolve to serve different purposes. As adult culture has embraced Facebook as a way to connect with a larger social group, many youth have moved their participation to a more private venue, primarily using the chat function Facebook provides, to stay connected with peers as an instant messaging (IM) tool (personal youth interviews, 2015). For many youth, the most important opportunities that this media offers for building and maintaining social relationships is hanging out (boyd, 2014).

Another function of new media is the control youth have over the communication they send out, and the public persona they create. When communicating via texts or IM, the youth have time to carefully craft their messages, even tweaking spelling and punctuation to convey an image (boyd, 2014). This also allows youth to manage their vulnerability in social interactions, as they have more control over those interactions. They also have more control over how they present themselves to their peers, as they choose what to share, how to share it, who to share it with, and have time to consider all of these different facets before posting or responding to others (boyd, 2014). Youth are able to create a public image through the photos they post on social media sites (Facebook, Instagram), edited videos (YouTube), or the popular culture they want to be associated with as a fan (Tumblr).

New media culture has largely been studied from an ethnographic lens. This allows researchers to consider questions within their social and cultural contexts (boyd, 2014; Ito et al., 2013). As my own approach is situationally based within the contextual model of learning and how people learn through the personal, physical, and socio-cultural lenses, this field reflects my theoretical lens.

5   Narrative of Context

5.1   *The New Media Maker Experience: Pixel Arts Game Education*

Pixel Arts Game Education is a program founded in 2013 in Portland, Oregon by two game enthusiasts who wanted to find ways to introduce more youth to game design experiences. Their motto is "play>make>design" and their mission is to help bridge the digital divide and reduce barriers of access to technology education by providing tools, resources, and mentoring support for game creation, focusing their attention on youth, particularly underserved youth in and around the region. They work primarily with libraries and schools to create game design opportunities of varying lengths and intensities. However, these "camps" as they are called, are all focused on building skills, both digital and social, that will enable youth to create games with others. According to game designers working with Pixel Arts, the majority of computer games are created by teams of people who work collaboratively, so engaging in these cooperative experiences is critical (personal notes, Pixel Arts volunteer training, January 2015).

To accomplish these goals, Pixel Arts emphasizes team building experiences, demonstrating through concrete examples that more creative solutions are developed by groups than an individual working alone. Collaborative creative experiences, such as group drawings or group authored short stories, are used to quickly and effectively demonstrate the divergent thinking of such group efforts.

The Pixel Arts team also wants youth to develop a growth mindset, based on Dweck's work on fixed versus growth mindsets (Dweck, 2012). Therefore, there are explicit and repeated messages about how skills such as art are developed over time, and that everyone improves with practice. They clearly address student insecurities about their artistic, programming, or other abilities, and give examples from their own lives about how they improved certain skills with attention and practice. The program emphasizes the difference between self-esteem and self-efficacy, and mentors are encouraged to use language that supports the development of the latter (personal notes, Pixel Arts volunteer training, January 2015). This also supports a growth mindset orientation for individuals in the group.

Based on motivational studies by Baumeister and others (2005), the premise of Pixel Arts is that experiences that build self-efficacy will naturally lead to self-esteem, and the language used with youth can encourage this process. Feedback is specific, "I like how you figured out how to get that character to jump that direction", rather than, "That is awesome!"

They also emphasize the social development of participating youth. One way in which they do that is through the co-creation of "rules" for behavior with participants. At the first session of each of the Pixel Arts camps, youth are asked to generate examples of how to "be safe", "respectful", "responsible", and to "do your best together", and then the group discusses these ideas and agrees to act in those ways. In short, Pixel Arts wants youth to experience a collaborative setting that respects collective memory, relationship building, cooperative activity, and the belief that all individuals have something to contribute. Youth are also encouraged to step into mentorship roles after participating in the camps, helping newer, more novice youth.

The Pixel Arts game education camp offered to the youth in this study was a nine-week, hour and a half, after-school program, included as part of the extra-curricular programming at the middle school. The following topics were explored: character creation, story design, art, music, and coding. Mentors gave information in short presentations, usually five to ten minutes in length. The skills were broken into small, manageable amounts of information and then the youth were given prompts or challenges (rather than assignments) to start working with the ideas. For example, in Week 3, the participating youth were introduced to the computer programming website, Scratch. The facilitator showed youth how to create a new scene, and move a character, called a Sprite, in four directions. Then the participants were encouraged to choose a Sprite from the Scratch library, move it, and add sound. After twenty minutes of exploration, the facilitator called the group back together to introduce how making a "loop" in which the character repeats the movement as a shortcut rather than repeating the same commands in the programming screen (author's notes and observations, 2015). The complexity of the experience comes through the activity of the youth.

Typically, these prompts or challenges were offered in ways that provide the learners with an element of choice, so they can explore the skills in ways that draw on their individual interests. These qualities increase the relevance of the experience and the autonomy of the participants. They are given choice and time to practice. The interests of the group as a whole can also be taken into consideration. The order of the skills presented in Pixel Arts programs varies, whenever possible, depending on what the group is most inspired to learn about. During the initial planning, the last few sessions are also left undesigned to let the group have some agency over what their final projects will entail.

Youth are also offered a lot of freedom about what kinds of games they can create. There is no judgment expressed by the adults and mentors for any ideas. This modeling helps create a supportive, inclusive environment where the youth respect each other's interests and goals as well. The limitations to game choices were only physical limitations, such as time and technology. One example is 3D modeling, which was beyond the scope of the time frame of this camp.

The author participated in this experience primarily as an observer, but also as an adult mentor to offer support around behavior and classroom management. As part of a larger, longitudinal study being conducted at the school, the author spent time on campus as a researcher and community coordinator for STEM activities so also played administrative roles for the group, taking attendance and acting as a liaison with the school for tech support as needed. The author has no expertise in game design, so did not offer support with the main activities of the club.

6   Practical Methods/Applications of Idea or Approach

6.1   *Authentic Spaces and Tools*
As guests, bringing an outside program into this middle school, Pixel Arts did not have complete control over the physical setting. However, from their earliest meeting with the after-school programming staff, they clearly

communicated that they did not want a conventional classroom setting, where all of the youth were facing the "front" of a space, and separated into individual spaces. It was important to them, and their program, that youth could arrange the space in ways that allowed them to work collaboratively on their game designs. They wanted the youth to experience this as an authentic game design setting.

The school moved into a brand-new building the previous summer and the architects were intentional about designing for learning environments. Both the computer lab at the school, where students take computer classes during the day and the media center used by Pixel Arts were configured such that youth are oriented towards each other and chairs are movable to allow youth to easily work together.

Another important factor in the physical context is the tools, particularly that the tools were authentic to the game design experience. One obvious tool is the desktop computers available to the youth in the media center. However, it also includes the software tools the Pixel Arts game design program introduced to the youth, as these tools allowed the youth to gain more mastery in an area of their own personal interest. This made the tools highly relevant to the youth, increased their agency, and made this game design experience authentic. The youth were learning "real" tools to make a "real" game. Programs introduced to the youth over the nine weeks of the session include: Scratch for game design, Pixlr for drawing/graphic design, BeepBox for music/soundtracks, and Bfxr.net for sound effects. Beyond this, there was explicit instruction on how to use resources such as Google to get further information about the tools and how to use them more effectively. In Week 4, a game that had been created at a recent "game jam" was shared with the youth where other local hobbyist and professional game designers had used many of the tools shared in Pixel Arts. As the youth saw the game and heard the soundtrack, they saw how the tools they interacted with in their after-school setting could be used by a team of game designers to create a playable game.

7 Implications for Learning Sites

The qualities of a Maker experience encompass qualities common in Free-Choice learning settings; they are interest driven, experiential, often collaborative, and process, not product, oriented. These are spaces where individuals share their questions, expertise, mistakes, and successes to create a community of like-minded, supportive peers of all ages and backgrounds. It is an experience that is available to all learners of all ages, no matter what kind of school or home education environment in which they find themselves. Maker activities can happen in a variety of settings. Activities range from game design and e-textiles to creating cardboard arcades- and anything in between. Materials can include purchased kits or repurposed objects. With the abundance of information on the internet, as well as resources already present in every community, such as books in the library or a neighbor around the corner, anyone can learn how to do most anything; no project is out of the reach of a learner. Since the tools and resources of a Maker experience can be found for little or no cost, the access issue becomes less of a concern. The qualities that Maker settings embody encourage identity work and growth along individual interest trajectories and these qualities can be implemented in a wide-variety of learning settings. Maker experiences can be made available for all learners. However, not everyone currently has access to these resources.

The Maker movement is different from many youth programs because, when done well (as observed in this study), it includes attributes which positively support youth development: intentional use of (1) a non-hierarchical facilitation style, (2) authentic tools and practices, (3) collaboration, (4) interest-driven activity and, (5) choice. These were critical to supporting youth agency, interest development and identity exploration around technology. These are strategies and principles that could be used in other alternative education settings.

Here are some ideas for creating a space that encourages this kind of learning, in either formal or informal settings:
- Flexible seating arrangements you can rearrange to create small group, large group, or individual seating.
- Space and tools for brainstorming, planning, designing (e.g., a white board type space that learners can use).
- Space/storage system to keep projects that may take multiple days. For computer designed games, art, writing, etc.; a common folder that is accessible to the group for storage can serve this purpose.
- Opportunities for learners to explore their own ideas, interests, questions, solutions.
- A culture that celebrates the process, not just the end product; make it explicitly okay to try more than once, to take a "finished" product and make it more efficient or aesthetic.
- Ways to document progress on a project, such as taking screen shots of game settings, progress journals, digital photographs of intermittent steps and more!
- Tools and resources that have easy entry points, but can encompass a variety of levels of expertise as the learners gain skills and knowledge.
- An acknowledgement that all members of the community have something to contribute so that roles of teacher/learner can flow in many directions.

- Adults willing to play the role of guide or facilitator more than the sole source of information or the gate-keeper of resources for the group.
- Events to celebrate progress and let learners share what they have done in a show and tell rather than competition setting.

While there is some concern that the Maker movement is elitist, the movement in and of itself is not elitist. Because of where these spaces are often located and the resources that are perceived as necessary for high end tools, more middle class and upper-class individuals and families are aware of them and what one can do in them. However, my findings demonstrate that youth from marginalized communities benefitted greatly from the opportunity to engage in one kind of Maker experience. As educators and researchers concerned with interest development, identity work, and deepening of understanding, we need to try harder to ensure that youth in under-resourced communities have those opportunities. Currently, school and community librarians are among those most passionate about providing spaces for youth to access Maker experiences and tools.

The Pixel Arts game design program was offered at a conventional public middle school, as part of an after-school program and in a space already present at the school. There is evidence that this 9- week program contributed to youths' interest development, identity exploration, and understanding of technology and technology-based careers. Thus, the implication is that Free-Choice Learning principles can be present in all types of settings. With subtle changes to the space and social relationships, a different learning experience was possible for the participants in this experience. These youths had the opportunity to explore their own interests, learn from their peers, and collaboratively create games as well as a learning environment.

8   Conclusions

Identity is a fluid concept, maybe more so during adolescence than at any other time in life. While Hidi and Renninger's four phases of interest development offer insight into the trajectories individuals may progress along, their work does not offer examples of what the accompanying identity development might look like. Therefore, using the actions of the youth as identified by Ito et al. (2013), their genres of participation as an expression of the youths' identities, I could analyze markers of identity transformation. There is evidence that during this 9-week experience, many of the youth progressed along a continuum during their experiences in Pixel Arts from "hanging out", to "messing around", to "geeking out". They used new media to find ways to express themselves and use technology in creative rather than consumptive ways.

References

Azevedo, F. S. (2011). Lines of practice: A practice-centered theory of interest relationships. *Cognition and Instruction, 29*(2), 147–184.

Baumeister, R. F. (2005). *The cultural animal: Human nature, meaning, and social life.* New York, NY: Oxford University Press.

boyd, d. (2014). *It's complicated: The social lives of networked teens.* New Haven, CT: Yale University Press.

Dweck, C. S. (2012). *Mindset.* London: Robinson.

Falk, J. H. (2001). *Free-choice science education: How we learn science outside of school.* New York, NY: Teachers College Press.

Falk, J. H., & Dierking, L. D. (2000). *Learning from museums: Visitor experiences and the making of meaning.* Walnut Creek, CA: AltaMira Press.

Falk, J. H., & Dierking, L. D. (2010). The 95 percent solution: School is not where most Americans learn most of their science. *American Scientist, 98*(6), 486–491.

Falk, J. H., & Dierking, L. D. (2011). *The museum experience.* Walnut Creek, CA: Left Coast Press.

Hidi, S., & Renninger, K. A. (2006). The four-phase model of interest development. *Educational Psychologist, 41*(2), 111–127.

Horst, H. A., Herr-Stephenson, B., & Robinson, L. (2013) Media ecologies. In M. Ito, S. Baumer, M. Bittanti, d. boyd, R. Cody, B. Herr-Stephenson, ... S. Yardi (Eds.), *Hanging out, messing around, and geeking out: Kids living and learning with new media.* Cambridge, MA: MIT Press.

Ito, M., Baumer, S., Bittanti, M., boyd, d., Cody, R., Herr-Stephenson, B., ... Yardi, S. (2013). *Hanging out, messing around, and geeking out: Kids living and learning with new media.* Cambridge, MA: MIT Press.

Renninger, K. A. (2009). Interest and identity development in instruction: An inductive model. *Educational Psychologist, 44*(2), 105–118.

Renninger, K. A., & Hidi, S. (2002). Interest and achievement: Developmental issues raised by a case study. In A. Wigfield & J. Eccles (Eds.), *Development of achievement motivation* (pp. 173–195). New York, NY: Academic Press.

Tai, R. H., Liu, C. Q., Maltese, A. V., & Fan, X. (2006). Planning early for careers in science. *Science, 312*, 1143–1144.

Thomas, D., & Seely Brown, J. (2011). *A new culture of learning: Cultivating the imagination for a world of constant change.* Lexington, KY: CreateSpace.

Worsley, M., & Blikstein, P. (2013). *Designing for diversely motivated learners.* Paper presented at the Digital Fabrication and Making in Education Workshop at the 2013 Interactive Design for Children Conference (IDC 2013), New York, NY.

CHAPTER 3

Digital Literacy Practices for a Gaming Generation: Commercial Gaming Lessons from Adolescent Gamers

Jason A. Engerman, Robert Hein, Nate Turcotte and Alison Carr-Chellman

1 Overarching Questions

1. How do adolescent boys experience and think about narrative-driven videogames?
2. Why might teachers want to consider integrating videogames or discussions about videogames into their classrooms?
3. How can teachers plan and conduct lessons based on student-interest in popular, commercial-off-the-shelf titles like *Assassin's Creed*, *Portal*, and *Uncharted*?
4. How can teachers navigate the controversial, "hot-button" issues surrounding videogames that so often find themselves focus of media scrutiny?
5. Likewise, what practical complications and challenges might teachers encounter as they move to implement games-based or games-inspired lessons?

2 Introduction

Commercial videogames have quickly become a dominant form of entertainment (Gartner, 2013). Consequently, videogame play has impacted the family household, with parents adapting to its popularity and ubiquity. Entertainment Software Association (ESA) statistics indicate that:
- 67% of parents play videogames with their child at least once a week
- 71% of parents say videogames have a positive influence on their child's life
- 94% of parents say they pay attention to the content (ESA, 2017, p. 4).

Not only does the ESA's (2017) data show that many parents play games with their children, but it also suggests that gaming provides a good opportunity to socialize with them (ESA, 2017). Given this rising popularity and household engagement, historical and cultural norms are forming around gameplay experiences. Thus, videogames can be viewed as historical artifacts that have become integral parts of our modern popular culture. Today, educators are exploring how commercial games-based learning approaches can leverage cultural knowledge that commercial games have fostered over time (Engerman, 2016) while using unique methods that disrupt the power dynamics of traditional classrooms. Commercial-off-the-shelf (COTS) games-based learning requires that students take the stage as experts and customize their learning experiences. COTS approaches could provide mutually beneficial outcomes for both learners and educators—particularly for disengaged learners in traditional school settings. For example, scholars have found that gaming can help improve New Literacy skills, particularly for boys (Abrams, 2009; Engerman, Yan, Mun, & Carr-Chellman, 2015; Gerber, 2009; Steinkuehler, 2011). This chapter will discuss boy gaming culture and its connections to New Literacy development. More specifically, the authors provide a theoretical frame within a four-year study on adolescent boys and their commercial gaming communities. Building on this framework, the chapter discusses practical methods and applications for educators while also highlighting challenges and concerns. Furthermore, the chapter provides additional resources and concludes with final thoughts on using videogames as tools for literacy development.

3   Boys, Video Games and Literacy

Mortenson (2011) highlights that boys are far more likely to be labeled emotionally disturbed, become homeless, land in a correctional facility, or end up dead between the ages of 15 and 24. These troubling disparities bring to rise the notion of a "boy crisis" (Sommers, 2013). Specifically, scholars highlight the ways in which our educational systems ignore the unique socio-cultural needs of boys (Steinkuehler, 2011; Yun, Mun, Engerman & Carr-Chellman, 2017). Not surprisingly, boys have historically—and disproportionately—struggled to engage in classroom lessons, achieve academic success, and develop literacy skills (Calderon & Lopez, 2013; Voyer & Voyer, 2014). Boys continue to underperform in these areas both domestically (U.S.) (Watson, Kehler, & Martino, 2010) and abroad (OECD, 2014). Consequently, these alienated boys come to reject school culture (Carr-Chellman, 2011).

Today, videogames—and the communities that form around them—play important sociocultural roles for young people. Although boys and girls now play videogames relatively equally (ESA, 2017), videogame play has been a particularly well-established pastime for boys (Cassell & Jenkins, 1998; Ragusa,

2014). Boys are much more likely to play videogames than beginning homework, and they treat gaming as a primary hobby when compared to girls (Phan, Jardnina, & Hoyle, 2012; Ragusa, 2014). Furthermore, games-based research suggests that girls play very different kinds of games than boys (Yee, 2006). Girls are more likely to play games within the Social, Puzzle/Card, Music/Dance, Educational/Edutainment, and Simulation genres (Phan et al., 2012). Furthermore, videogames facilitate aggressive and competitive interactions that boys historically gravitate towards (Cassell & Jenkins, 1998; Engerman, 2016). Subsequently, work in educational psychology (Kindlon & Thomas, 2009; Sax, 2007) leads us to see gaming as the modern and natural progression of activities such as roughhousing or pickup basketball. More directly, we are interested in boys and their technological practices within their indigenous social environments. By *indigenous*, we mean the native and natural social habitat of these young learners. Thus, particular videogames have become part of adolescent boy culture (Engerman et al., 2015). However, these more natural types of engagements are shunned by the general public—particularly within traditional school settings.

Gaming scholars have suggested that video games provide literacy experiences and can even improve New Literacy skills (Gee, 2000; Gerber & Abrams, 2014). According to Gee (2000), New Literacies actively recruit distinctive oral and written social languages for learning. Furthermore, these languages are situated within socioculturally recognizable and meaningful discourses. With the aforementioned boy educational gaps in mind, we argue that classroom teachers should recognize these indigenous commercial gaming environments as powerful educational tools. In the following section we discuss the theoretical frame and literature that guided our investigation.

4   Theoretical Frame and Literature Review

Our on-going study represented the culmination of a four-year investigation of the lived experiences of video-game-playing adolescent boys. We aimed to uncover the intentionality and meaning-making processes within the game play of our participants. We utilized Cultural Historical Activity Theory (CHAT) to gain greater insight on the value and impact of their practices through unpacking both conscious and subconscious motivations, passions, and desires that encourage them to engage in social and cultural activities (Engestrom, 1987). CHAT—which is rooted in Social Development Theory (Vygotsky, 1978)—takes on a holistic approach that seeks out meaning-making through symbolic instruments in the gaming environment. Thus, our sociocultural framework looks at activity systems and their mediating factors to make sense of the boys' active learning experiences (Engestrom, 1987). Sociocultural approaches such as CHAT aligns with understanding new age literacy practices. A syncretic approach to understanding literacy examines the interdependent relationship between individuals and the social worlds in which they live (Gutierrez, Bien, & Selland, 2011). Similar to a syncretic approach, we begin with a particular social problem in boy alienation in traditional schools; we acknowledge the complexity, historical relevance, and embedded multilevel context (Gutierrez et al., 2011). Not only do syncretic approaches on literacy utilize cultural and historical relevance, but they also recognize that literacy practices are part of overlapping and interwoven social phenomena across time and space (Gutierrez et al., 2011). Therefore, syncretic literacy approaches emphasize an analysis of the learners and their movements across their daily routines (Guiterrez, 2008).

Several scholars have explored video game play and its connections to literacy skills and development. James Gee is a well-known linguistic scholar and games-based-learning champion. In a massively open online course, Gee outlined 13 learning principles embedded in good games. Among these, Gee emphasized that meaning-making occurs through active, embodied engagement with language-based symbols ("Meaning as Action", 2013). He emphasized the impact that active engagement has on meaning-making practices and literacy gains. Theoretical work, such as Gee's, provides the framework for others, like Constance Steinkuehler, to conduct comprehensive studies on the connections between gaming and learning. For example, Steinkuehler's (2007) ethnographic work on massively multiplayer online games (MMOGs)—like *World of Warcraft* and *Lineage*—explored how gamers constantly engage in "literacy activities" ranging from text-based communication and reading to the creation and maintenance of fan websites. Figure 3.1 shows an example of in-game readings from *World of Warcraft*. Steinkuehler has since taken a closer look at how boys—in particular—use these online spaces to practice and experiment with digital "modding" and writing practices. Steinkuehler's (2011) study on "The Mismeasure of Boys" revealed that games-based learning lead to a 17% increase in self-correction rates on reading comprehension tasks among her adolescent boy participants.

Based on Steinkuhler's (2011) work, engagement in reading is closely linked to both autonomy and interest. Morphing literacies refers to how learners adapt their in-school activities into more socially acceptable and meaningful literacies (Blair & Sanford, 2004). The boys in Blair and Sanford's study attempted to shape the events in their daily lives to duplicate times and experiences where they are natively immersed. In other words, boys would transform schoolwork into applicable components for their social lives according to their interests

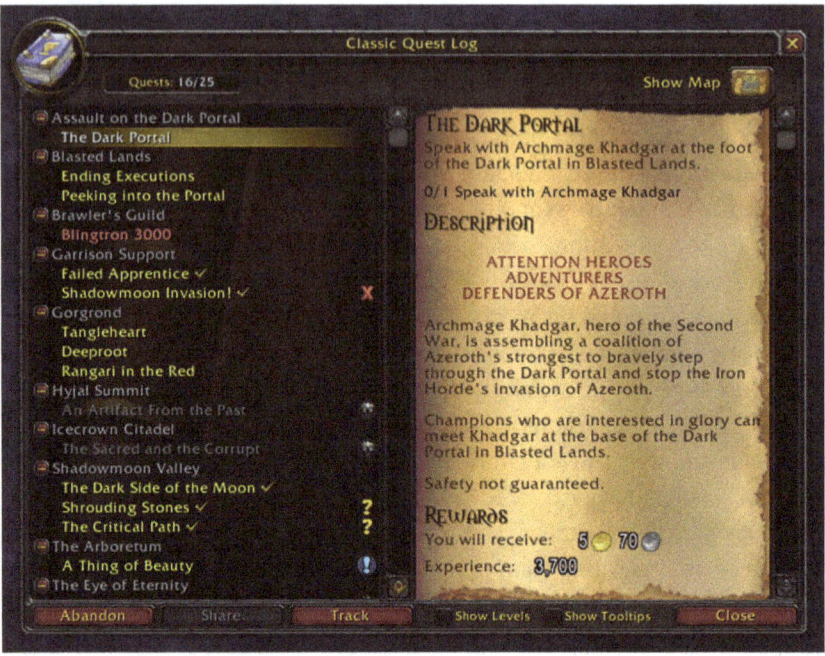

FIGURE 3.1   In-game text in *World of Warcraft*

and towards building cultural capital among peers. As a result, these boy learners were more likely to read and interact with material that could later be leveraged as tools to socialize with friends. The findings of this study suggest that boys can practice new literacy skills when presented with texts that align with their cultural values and social ambitions (Blair & Sanford, 2004). Although it is clear that boys morph their literacies in this way, little work has been done to understand *how* these transformations occur. With action and interest-driven examples, we feel there may be a unique place for games in traditional school settings. After all, as scholars note, video games can be viewed as "texts" that encourage new forms of reading and writing (Gee, 2007; Jones & Hafner; 2012). As such, our study may help inform the larger field by beginning to explain the historical and social influences around the culture of video game play. We continue with a narrative of our context to elaborate on conditions of our study.

5   Narrative of Context

In order to better understand their nuanced culture and relationships with videogames, we selected a group of boys to engage in a phenomenological study of learning in games. For over four years The Pennsylvania State University

Learning, Design and Technology research team, directed by Dr. Carr-Chellman and led by Dr. Engerman, has followed a population of 24 adolescent boys to dissect their relationships with COTS games. This becomes particularly relevant considering the normalized negative stigma of video-game-playing boys. The study consisted of deep phenomenological investigations, through a sociocultural and historic lens (Engestrom, 1987) into the meaning of the COTS gaming experiences for boy culture (Engerman et al., 2015). The study emphasized both the conscious and subconscious impacts and meaning-making practices of videogame culture on boy adolescent development including their perceptions, motivations, emotions, desires, and embodied actions (Stanford Encyclopedia, 2016). The research team discovered ties to the Common Core Standards in English Language Arts and Social Studies/History literacy, 21st Century Learning skills, as well as the International Society for Technology in Education (ISTE) standards (Engerman et al., 2015). As the emphasis of this study focused on student voice, we narrate these voices through participant pseudonyms according to IRB specifications.

Fellow educators and librarians have contacted our research team to inquire about suggestions for COTS use in traditional classrooms, including insights into curriculum development. In response to this need in the educational community, the Learning and Performance Systems department asked Dr. Carr-Chellman to develop a Gaming2Learn course through Pennsylvania State's World Campus. Gaming2Learn provides educators with practical applications of games-based learning and helps educators develop COTS-inspired lessons for their own classrooms. In the following sections, we will not only share two samples of practical, games-based approaches, but we will also provide commentary on the challenges facing their implementation.

6 Pedagogical Methods of Ideas or Approaches

6.1 *Assassin's Creed (AC) and Critical Reading*

Assassin's Creed is a popular videogame series that is known for its detailed, engaging, and authentic historical settings. Players adopt the roles of various time-traveling assassins as they explore the likes of Renaissance-era Italy and revolutionary New England. As players complete the game's missions, they slowly work to unravel mysteries and conspiracies that have been centuries in the making. Along the way, they often gather clues by reading in-game notes, letters, and journals. Our participants believed that reading these texts enhanced their understanding of both history and vocabulary words, motivating them to learn more about those topics in the classroom.

Interviewer: Could you kind of describe what the text looks like in the game?

Brad: There's a biography piece for Leonardo da Vinci, and it went into how he was a painter and then he sort of got into architecture and art-related architecture and building things. And it told about how he was not really accepted by anybody until after he was dead and how he was sort of was like in the shadows all the time. The religious figures didn't like him because he didn't rely on religion. He relied on science which is the reason a lot of people didn't like him back then until after his death.

...

Interviewer: Do you think that reading the text in the game had prepared you to read text in the classroom at all?

Brad: Uh...yes actually, because a lot of my history class in high school was American History. Also, a lot of Civil War stuff. I learned that earlier before I played the *Assassin's Creed* game about the Revolutionary War and that's what I mean. The Civil War, the Revolutionary War. I had learned it before I started playing the game and when I played the game I recognized some of the stuff I had actually paid attention to in the classroom and I actually probably learned more from the game than I would have in class.

We can see from Brad's responses that the game space had a significant impact on his understanding of the material for class. His embodied actions within the game as well as the digital reading materials helped to provide deep engagement as well as retention. Meaning-making occurs through active, embodied engagement with language-based symbols ("Meaning is Action", 2013). Narrative and history-driven videogames like *Assassin's Creed* offer this elevated form of engagement because words are immediately translated into actions (Gee, 2007). Educators could place particular emphasis on the historical time frames, the rich culture, the architecture, political dynamics, and/or sociological interactions.

6.2   *Assassins Creed II (M) and the 7–9 History/Social Studies Class*

We carried the previous views into the preparation of the following conceptual lesson. To engage in critical reading, students could participate in a project-based learning assignment. Students could pretend to be reporters working at a news station that uses a time-travel device to journey back to Renaissance Italy. However, instead of using just their imaginations, students could play through several predetermined sections of *Assassin's Creed*. In *Assassin's Creed II,* players stumble across Leonardo da Vinci as he completes his Mona Lisa

FIGURE 3.2   Assassin's Creed II

(see Figure 3.2)—they have the opportunity to *actually* talk to him as they *actually* visit and explore the Sistine Chapel.

Educators could center on curriculum standards to enforce textual and verbal language as students explore the virtual world. Students could then engage the game with an eye towards satisfying several *PA Standards The Common Core State Standards (Reading Historical Informational Text)* (NGA & CCCSSO, 2015) including:

- (CCSS.ELA-LITERACY.RH.6-8.2) Determine the central ideas or information of a primary or secondary source; provide an accurate summary of the source distinct from prior knowledge or opinions.
- (CCSS.ELA-LITERACY.RH.6-8.3) Identify key steps in a text's description of a process related to history/social studies (e.g., how a bill becomes law, how interest rates are raised or lowered).
- (CCSS.ELA-LITERACY.RH.6-8.7) Integrate visual information (e.g., in charts, graphs, photographs, videos, or maps) with other information in print and digital texts.
- (CCSS.ELA-LITERACY.RH.6-8.8) Distinguish among fact, opinion, and reasoned judgment in a text.

Using a primary text to guide the factual information, an educator could leverage the developers' creative liberties to engage in "teachable moments". Teachers could use these opportunities to help students distinguish fact from creative fiction. It is important to remember, however, that games like *Assassin's Creed* are inherently violent. Of course, that is precisely why so many of our students enjoy them. As we have already suggested, boys, in particular, are drawn to violent fantasy play and aggressive competition in games (Engerman,

2016; Newkirk, 2002). Depending on a teacher's understanding of the game and, as Engerman (2016) notes, of their own playography–a player's digitally historical play biography or play identity–(Mitgutsch, 2013), teachers could provide specific objectives for students to complete. Conversely, this might be an opportunity for the teacher to step back and allow the students to develop their own mechanisms for meeting the aforementioned standards. Notions such as these flip the power dynamics and place more responsibility on the student. A reasonable assessment for this type of assignment might be an open-ended writing assignment in which learners are able to express their experiences comparing and contrasting textbook facts from the ones that the game provides. These conceptual lessons were aggregated and presented at the Pennsylvania Educational Technology Expo and Conference (Engerman & Carr-Chellman, 2014). More conceptual lessons are listed within Appendix A for further review. In addition, the research team utilized these ideas to formulate a graduate-level course around commercial game-based learning for teacher development entitled "Gaming2Teach".

6.3 *Gaming2Teach*

Gaming2Teach is not a game design course, but instead a course that focuses on applying gaming to learning contexts across K-12, corporate, non-profit, and informal learning spaces. Introducing game-based learning methods in traditional public schools is a difficult task. The previously mentioned critical reading and History Standards also guided user-experience and innovative use of digital game-based environments within our Gaming2Learn course. We utilized our research to inform our selection of materials and our reconceptualization of learner experiences. In our course design, it was important to explore the complications that might arise for each COTS implementation. Are districts, parents, administrators, policy makers, and other students willing to allow teachers to bring COTS games into the classroom? This course was inspired by the gaps in learning that we observed in the literature but also driven by our discoveries of the power of indigenous learning environments, particularly COTS videogames. The course represents a traditional 15-week semester-long examination of the gaming-for-learning industry from educational games to COTS games. The assignments ranged from assessments of readings to discussions on the values of different kinds of learning in gaming environments, as well as the integration of a single game into a single content area through a lesson-planning document. The heart of the course focused on the application of gaming for the purposes of learning in traditional classroom environments. The ultimate goal of Gaming2Teach seeks to harness a growing relationship between teachers and game integration in effective, efficient, and fun ways.

6.4   Concerns May Rise

Of course, non-traditional lessons or interventions—like the ones we suggest here—should be approached with some amount of trepidation. Despite a growing body of research and literature that highlights their educational affordances, videogames still occasionally find themselves being demonized by media outlets that choose to fixate on their violent natures. That said, we urge teachers to examine and evaluate modern games based on their academic content and built-in learning principles. After all, we teach Shakespearean tragedies and American history despite their bloody moments. Perhaps we should not treat videogames like *Assassin's Creed*, which challenge students both intellectually and creatively, any differently. While the violent and competitive nature of videogames raises issues directly related to the classroom acceptance of gaming, there are also some concerns from non-media sources as well; for example, teacher time, breadth of curriculum coverage, incorrect information propagated by games, and classroom competitiveness can be brought into question in the face of serious gaming in the classroom.

Another issue could potentially foil even the most well-designed games-based lessons is that of access. Even if teachers *want* to take up our challenge, school districts might not be able to lend the necessary support. Although the cost of these games and consoles has dropped over time, it still might not be economically feasible for students to play through entire games individually. Although some students already play these games in their homes, others simply cannot. How, then, do teachers bridge this digital divide? One strategy might be to set up a console and projector in the classroom where students can take turns playing and watching particular sections of a game. Through collectively experiencing the game as a class, teachers could provide just-in-time information or ask open-ended questions for group discussions. This strategy also draws on the growing popularity of videogame-live streaming culture and machinima production—where players describe, in the moment, why and how they are completing certain tasks in their virtual environment. Through this process, the students playing the games could make their thinking and problem-solving visible for classmates (Hein & Engerman, 2016).

Ultimately, for teachers, the key is to tackle games-based lessons with open eyes, with a clear vision of how they want to use games, and what the potential problems may be that come with the use of COTS videogames in classrooms. Some of the problems have been outlined already—teacher time, finances, equity, competitiveness, violence, parent/administrator approvals, sufficient classroom time to cover all the needed content, incorrect information that may be spread by game play are all examples of things that teachers need to prepare for if they decide to engage games for learning in their own classrooms. To get the most out of games like *Assassin's Creed, Portal,* or *Uncharted,* teachers need to be prepared to respond to complications from technology failures to outraged parents. Most importantly, perhaps, teachers need to be willing to play through the games for themselves and to spend a good deal of time really learning a new game and linking it to learning goals. Today's teachers might not consider themselves "gamers", but they may find that engaging alienated learners on their own cultural grounds may allow them to better connect with and instruct the coming generation of students.

7 Conclusion

This chapter reviewed the links between social gaming spaces and the New Literacy practices being developed at the intersection of boy culture and commercial game play. When considering educational technology integration, we should look beyond more traditional and instruction-centered technologies. Syncretic literacy approaches, like the one mentioned here, focus on learners and on their movements across daily routines and captures deep sociocultural meaning making connections (Guiterrez, 2008). We should seek indigenous knowledge spaces and learner-centered tools. Too often policy-makers, administrators, and even educators have dictated students' educational pathways. As a result of this coercive learning approach (Carr-Chellman, 2011; Kohn, 2000), schools have discouraged boys from pursuing their interests and personal learning goals. These traditional curricular policies, and their often questionable application, have left little opportunity for learners to explore their own meaning-making processes in normal and natural ways. New literacies–such as modern videogames and their virtual environments–encourage users to become active participants in the consumption and production of knowledge (Gee, 2000). Historically, boys have appropriated videogame spaces for use as social spaces (Engerman, 2016; Ragusa, 2014). Within their peer cultures, boys have developed sophisticated ways to make meaning in videogame spaces. These indigenous learning environments may play a vital role in the development of needed literacy skills for the 21st-century (Gee, 2000). As previously mentioned, games like *Assassins Creed II* provide players with an ability to *actually* engage directly with a historical experience. Commercial games have the potential to influence the ways in which educators think about digital spaces and learning.

In alignment with games-based learning literature, videogames undoubtedly afford learning opportunities (Engerman, 2016; Steinkuehler, 2011). The current study demonstrated how commercial games allow players an ability to determine the central ideas or information of a primary or secondary source;

provide an accurate summary of the source distinct from prior knowledge or opinions. These gaming environments are inclusive places for learners, and have the potential to provide a natural sense of comfort, as well as motivation. Videogames can be leveraged, not only to re-engage boy learners, but also to improve 21st-century skills for all learners (Engerman, at al., 2015). Gaming2Learn is a progressive attempt to enlighten teachers on the engagement and learning potential around gaming cultures. Teachers can leverage commercial games as educational technologies to help enhance classroom objectives as well as to re-engage learners. As a society, and particularly as educators, perhaps it is time to respect the cultural power of games and to create learning environments *with* learners, in order to provide authentic meaning-making opportunities. To accomplish this, we must begin by respecting indigenous digital peer cultures and include both the cultures and their learners in the processes of developing their own educational pathways.

Appendix A: Conceptual Uses for the K-12 Classroom[1]

In addition to our course development within Gaming2Learn, we conceptualized practical activities and lessons for the K-12 classroom. These lessons were inspired by Gee's (2013) notion of "situated meaning", which suggests learners cannot understand the meaning of words or symbols unless an association is made between an image, action, or experience. During this presentation we formulated generic lessons for three games discussed along concept, the Pennsylvania Student Aligned System (SAS), complications, and benefits (*Assassin's Creed*, *Uncharted*, and *God of War*). The primary purpose of these generic designs was to spark conversation and provide food for thought for practicing educators around the notions of leveraging commercial video games towards educational attainment.

Game 1: Assassins Creed II (M) and the 7–9 History/Social Studies Class

Assassins Creed represents a well-known series within the gaming community. *AC II* is situated during the Italian Renaissance and provides players with an immersive, engaging, and authentic environments to explore.

Concept. Developing critical reading and writing skills through Project-based learning. The educator could turn the classroom into a news station that has the ability to travel back in time. The students would then take on the role of reporters that travel back in time to Renaissance Italy working at a news station. The educator could assign journalistic roles as the students with signed permission slips to play the game (most likely from home). The journalist's primary role would be to gather information from the field and arrange the information in a summary. Also, the class would need editors, which would be students without the permission slips. The editor's major role would be to help the journalist refine and revise the information according to the editor-in-chief's (educator) specifications. Still other class members could become news anchors that would produce a video or finalized form of the information for the station to report out to the public.

Goal. The goal of this project could be on a deep dive into the historical time, the rich culture, the architecture, political dynamics, and/or social interactions of everyday Italians during the renaissance. Students could use a primary text to guide the factual information and provide an accurate account of the time period. The game serves as a time capsule in which learners can experience the ambience of the era in more tangible ways.

Learning Standards (Reading Informational Text)

(CC.8.5.6-8.B) Determine the central ideas or information of a primary or secondary source; provide an accurate summary of the source distinct from prior knowledge or opinions.

(CC.8.5.6-8.C) Identify key steps in a text's description of a process related to history/social studies (e.g., how a bill becomes law, how interest rates are raised or lowered).

(CC.8.5.6-8.G) Integrate visual information (e.g., in charts, graphs, photographs, videos, or maps) with other information in print and digital texts.

(CC.8.5.6-8.H) Distinguish among fact, opinion, and reasoned judgment in a text.

Consider This. Centered on curriculum objectives that reinforce textual and verbal language as the class explores the game, opportunities to dispel misconceptions can arise based on incorrect information within the game space. These fictional accounts are utilized by the developer's creative freedom to add variation and suspense to the narrative; they should be viewed as teachable moments and provide opportunities for students to think critically about their digital consumption. The game is violent in nature so take proper precautions with administrative and parental communication.

Complications. Complications may arise in terms of access, which can be mitigated by the use of various tools. *Twitch.tv* provides an open channel for students to observe other players via streaming, as well as recorded sessions. Teachers can screen these and provide videos that are appropriate for specific lessons. When considering these types of projects, a teacher may want to consider flipping the classroom, which turns the classroom into a workstation while allowing students to learn or gather information from home. Another option within the flipped classroom approach may be to ask students to develop machinima. Machinima is the use of real-time computer graphics engines to create video. Basically, videogame players record their gameplay. This can be used to capture particular aspects of the game as assigned by the teacher.

Game 2: Uncharted 3: Drakes Deception (T) for 9–10 English Language Arts (ELA Framework)

Uncharted is a well-known series and the third installment is particularly comparable to the famous Indiana Jones series. *Uncharted 3* provides incredibly cinematic properties that are compelling and rich for English Language arts development. This version has a softer rating for teen adolescents. Furthermore, *Uncharted 3* received some of the highest parental ratings on *Common Sense Media*.

Concept. Class Jigsaw for Writing/Speaking and Listening Uncharted Book 3

Phase 1
#1 Develop character profiles
#2 Develop scenery including locations
#3 Develop relationships between and amongst characters
#4 Provide a creative ending

Phase 2
#1 Revisions of elements
#2 Finalization of book

Goal. The goal of this book project could be to develop a tangible product and ignite creativity. Students would be engaging in Blooms final stage of his taxonomy in evaluation and creation. By engaging in the development of literary work students would participate and take charge of their own learning outcomes with physical products to add to their portfolios.

Learning Standards (Writing)
(CC.1.4.9–10.A) Write informative/explanatory texts to examine and convey complex ideas, concepts, and information clearly and accurately.

(CC.1.4.9–10.M) Write narratives to develop real or imagined experiences or events.

(CC.1.4.9–10.V) Conduct short as well as more sustained research projects to answer a question (including a self-generated question) or solve a problem; narrow or broaden the inquiry when appropriate; synthesize multiple sources on the subject, demonstrating understanding of the subject under investigation.

Complications. Finding the appropriate length of game play might be difficult as the game narrative and cinematic design requires much time to complete. Writing skills will be tested if the expectation is to produce a publishable product. Considering the lack of expectations on publishable products, student may become frustrated with the level and rigor and repetition to create a high-quality product. The benefits, however include incredible amounts of collaboration and strong narratives. Deep levels of critical thinking and authentic learning are possible.

Game 3: God of War II (M) and the 12 Grade Comparative Literature Class

God of War II can be considered the heart of the trilogy. The mechanics of the game are smooth and appealing. Lastly, *God of War II* can be technically demanding and requires a sophisticated level of expertise.

Concept. Literature Debate. A debate of this type will require deep levels of collaboration. In addition, students will need to be motivated and engage in multiliteracies including operational, cultural and operational (Sanford & Madill, 2007).

Goal. The goal of the debate will answer the question, "Does the *Percy Jackson* series capture Greek Mythology better than the video Game *God of War*?" Therefore, the primary emphasis of this debate will be for learners to justify and develop sophisticated levels of argumentation.

Debate Format
- *A Proposition* sets the stage. You begin with your side of the argument and stake a claim as to why that is within the appropriate section.
- *A Rebuttal* rebukes the claims that are made by the opposing team. Using their arguments as well as their evidence to position themselves.
- *A Cross Examination* allows the proposing team to respond. Using the opposing team's arguments or using new arguments.
- *A Second Rebuttal* allows the second team replies.
- *Closing Statements* close the statements made depending on the flow of the debate.

Learning Standards (Speaking and Listening)

(CC.1.5.11–12.A) Initiate and participate effectively in a range of collaborative discussions on grade-level topics, texts, and issues, building on others' ideas and expressing their own clearly and persuasively

(CC.1.5.11–12.C) Integrate multiple sources of information presented in diverse formats and media (e.g., visually, quantitative, orally) in order to make informed decisions and solve problems, evaluating the credibility and accuracy of each source and noting any discrepancies among the data.

(CC.1.5.11–12.D) Present information, findings, and supporting evidence, conveying a clear and distinct perspective; organization, development, substance, and style are appropriate to purpose, audience, and task

(CC.1.5.11–12.G) Demonstrate command of the conventions of standard English when speaking based on Grades 11–12 level and content.

Considerations

The Length could be about 1–2 months.

The Teams could have six to eight-member teams. Each team will need experts of the game, the book series, but everyone should be familiar primary source material for factual Greek mythology. Arrange teams such that *God of War* gamers are split evenly. They become the experts of the game and can guide their team through the elements of the game that would demonstrate their position.

Good Management could involve the need for teachers to establish ground rules that suit each classroom environment and established culture. Examples may include, #1: Argue within the topic focus, #2: Draw on the material to make all claims, or #3: Penalties.

Resources that could be used may be *God of War II*, *God of War II* books, Rick Riordan's *The Last Olympian*, *God of War II* machinima and online forums.

Complications may include time as it can become a major concern during this debate activity. Building towards the debate may take students time to prepare. Depend on how in depth the debate should be a teacher may one to consider expanding or contracting the scope of this activity. Mini debates may shorten preparation time.

Note

1 This presentation can be retrieved from bit.ly/MeetCCSS

References

Abrams, S. S. (2009). A gaming frame of mind: Digital contexts and academic implications. *Educational Media International, 46*(4), 335–347.

Blair, H. A., & Sanford, K. (2004). Morphing literacy: Boys reshaping their school-based literacy practices. *Language Arts, 81*(6), 452–460.

Carr-Chellman, A. (2011, January). *TedxPSU. Gaming to re-engage boys in learning.* Retrieved from http://www.ted.com/talks/gaming_to_re_engage_boys_in_learning.html

Cassell, J., & Jenkins, H. (1998). *From barbie to mortal kombat: Gender and computer games.* Cambridge, MA: MIT Press.

Engerman, J. A. (2016). *Call of duty for adolescent boys: An ethnographic phenomenology of the experiences within a gaming culture* (Doctoral dissertation). The Pennsylvania State University, Pennsylvania, PA. Retrieved from https://etda.libraries.psu.edu/catalog/t722h88oz

Engerman, J. A., & Carr-Chellman, A. (2014, February). *Meeting the common core with boys and games.* Concurrent session presented at the Pennsylvania Educational Technology Expo and Conference, Hershey, PA.

Engerman, J. A., Mun, Y., Yan, S., & Carr-Chellman, A. (2015). *Video games to engage boys and meet common core.* Research Paper Presentation International Society for Technology in Education (ISTE). Philadelphia, PA: International Society for Technology in Education.

Engeström, Y. (1987). *Learning by expanding: An activity-theoretical approach to developmental research.* Helsinki, Norway: Orienta-Konsultit.

Entertainment Sports Association. (2017). *Games: Improving education.* Retrieved from http://www.theesa.com/wp-content/uploads/2017/04/EF2017_FinalDigital.pdf

Gartner. (2013). *Global video game market expenditure from 2011 to 2015, by segment (in billion U.S. dollars).* Retrieved from http://www.statista.com/statistics/273597/global-video-game-market-expenditure/

Gee, J. P. (2000). The new literacy studies: From 'socially situated' to the work. In D. Barton, M. Hamilton, & R. Ivanic (Eds.), *Situated literacies: Reading and writing in context* (pp. 180–196). London: Routledge.

Gee, J. P. (2007). *What video games have to teach us about learning and literacy.* New York, NY: Palagrave MacMillan.

Gee, J. P. (2013, November). Gee principle 13 – Meaning as action. In *Video games & learning.* Retrieved from https://class.coursera.org/videogameslearning-001/wiki/week-one

Gerber, H. R. (2009). From the FPS to the RPG: Using video games to encourage reading YAL. *The ALAN Review, 36*(3).

Gerber, H. R., & Abrams, S. S. (2014). *Bridging literacies with videogames*. Rotterdam, The Netherlands: Sense Publishers.

Gutiérrez, K. D. (2008). Developing a sociocritical literacy in the third space. *Reading Research Quarterly, 43*(2), 148–164.

Gutierrez, K. D., Bien, A. C., & Selland, M. K. (2011). Syncretic approaches to studying movement and hybridity in literacy practices. In D. Lapp & D. Fisher (Eds.), *Handbook of research on teaching the English language arts*. New York, NY: Routledge.

Hein, R., & Engerman, J. A. (2016). Knowledge production in E-sports culture: Learning with and from the masters. In K. Valentine & L. Jensen (Eds.), *Examining the evolution of gaming and its impact on social, cultural, and political perspectives*. Hershey, PA: IGI Global.

Jones, R. H., & Hafner C. A. (2012). *Understanding digital literacies: A practical introduction*. New York, NY: Routledge.

Lopez, S., & Calderon, V. (2013). How American's boys become psychological dropouts. *The Gallup Blog*. Retrieved from http://www.gallup.com/opinion/gallup/171629/america-boys-become-psychological-245dropouts.aspx?utm_source=How%20American%E2%80%99s%20Boys%20Become%20Psychological%20Dropouts&utm_medium=search&utm_campaign=tiles

Mitgutsch, K. (2013). Why sports videogames matter to their players: Exploring meaningful experiences in playographies. In K. Mitgutsch, A. Stein, & M. Consalvo (Eds.), *Sports videogames* (pp. 253–277). New York, NY: Routledge.

National Governors Association & Council of Chief State School Officers. (2015). *Common core state standards initiative*. Retrieved from http://www.corestandards.org/ELA-Literacy/RH/6-8/8/

Newkirk, T. (2002). *Misreading masculinity: Boys, literacy, and popular culture*. Heinemann, 361 Hanover Street, Portsmouth, NH 03801-3912.

Phan, M. H., Jardina, J. R., Hoyle, S., & Chaparro, B. S. (2012, September). Examining the role of gender in video game usage, preference, and behavior. In *Proceedings of the human factors and ergonomics society annual meeting* (Vol. 56, Issue 1, pp. 1496–1500).

Ragusa, G. (2014). Gender, social media, games and the college landscape. In W. G. Tierney, Z. B. Corwin, T. Fullerton, & G. Ragusa (Eds.), *Postsecondary play: The role of games and social media in higher education*. Baltimore: John Hopkins University Press.

Stanford Encyclopedia of Philosophy. (2016). *Phenomenology*. Retrieved from http://plato.stanford.edu/entries/phenomenology/

Steinkuehler, C. (2007). Massively multiplayer online gaming as a constellation of literacy practices. *E-Learning and Digital Media, 4*(3), 297–318.

Steinkuehler, C. (2011). *The Mismeasure of boys: Reading and online videogames* (No. 2011- 3). WCER Working Paper.

Voyer, D., & Voyer, S. D. (2014). Gender differences in scholastic achievement: A meta-analysis. *Psychological Bulletin.* doi:10.1037/a0036620

Vygotsky, L. S. (1978). *Mind in society.* Cambridge, MA: Harvard University Press.

Yan, S., Mun, Y., Engerman, J. A., & Carr-Chellman, A. (2017). Boys and video game play: Re-engaging boys in the classroom. In R. Joseph, J. Moore, & A. Benson (Eds.), *Culture, learning and technology: Research and practice.* New York, NY: Taylor & Francis.

Yee, N. (2006). Motivations for play in online games. *CyberPsychology & Behavior, 9*(6), 772–775.

CHAPTER 4

Literacies of Play: Blazing the Trail, Unchartered Territories, and Hurrying Up – #TeamLaV's Interview with James Paul Gee

Raúl Alberto Mora, James Paul Gee, Michael Hernandez, Sebastián Castaño, Tyrone Steven Orrego and Daniel Ramírez

1 Overarching Questions

1. What should gaming researchers keep in mind to address the potential critiques of revisiting videogames in education?
2. How can the next generation of gamers-as-scholars make an impact beyond the traditional academic outlets?
3. What kinds of research avenues can we consider as we look at the intersection of videogames and second-language learning practices?
4. Looking at Gee's idea of G/game, what are the ethical challenges that videogames research must consider in the incoming decade?
5. Gee calls for a full paradigm shift in schools. How should videogames research in the immediate future heed that call?

2 Introduction

#TeamLaV, as part of the Literacies in Second Languages Project research initiative (Mora, 2015), has inquired about the nature of interactions that gamers who are second language users (Gaviria, 2018) engage in as part of their gaming experiences. Since 2014, our team is still inquiring about these different linguistic, semiotic, and aesthetic elements that lead to sustained commitment and success within the game experience. As has been the case with quite a few gaming researchers, one of the first authors we surveyed was James Paul Gee. As one of the original trailblazers in the field of videogames research, in addition to his influence in D/discourse analysis (Gee, 1999) and new literacies (Gee, 2008), Gee's work in gaming and literacy highlights how learners integrate social, culture and cognitive processes to make sense of the world.

Our readings of Gee's work became a source of inspiration for our first study (Mora, Castaño, Hernandez, Orrego, Ramírez, & Castaño, 2016; Mora, Castaño,

Orrego, Hernandez, & Ramírez, 2016), where we coined our evolving framework we have called "Language-as-Victory" or LaV (Hernandez & Castaño, 2015). Our idea of LaV and its current evolution (Mora, Castaño, Londoño-Mazo, Ramírez, Mazo, & Mejia, 2019) stemmed in no small part from Gee's idea that educators (all past and current #TeamLaV researchers are preservice or inservice teachers and Raúl is a teacher educator) need to look carefully at what is happening in videogames today and let some of those lessons permeate our classrooms.

As part of this volume, we had the incredible opportunity to interview James Gee and discuss with him the past and future of gaming research, as well as share our thoughts about our framework to see further inspiration from him as our research moves forward. We created the interview protocol that comprises this chapter, as all the things we do at #TeamLaV, as a team effort, a mission of sorts (Mora, Castaño, Gaviria, Londoño-Mazo, Mejía, & Ramírez, 2019). We created the protocol as an initial conversation between Sebastián, Tyrone, and Daniel (Michael, our second author, was in Egypt for his student teaching at the time). Once we agreed on the questions, Raúl interviewed Jim via Zoom on March 31, 2018. Michael, back from his student teaching, transcribed the interview in full.

We divided the interview into three sections: The first part (Blazing the Trail) revisits Gee's initial work and his one book that arguably broke the field of gaming research open, looking at its genesis and overall impact. The second part (Unchartered Territories) features some specific questions that Sebastián, Daniel, and Tyrone each asked Jim from their perspectives as seasoned gamers. Here, Raúl also mentioned the LaV framework to gain some insights from Jim and his thoughts about what #TeamLaV should consider next. Given that our framework takes into consideration the collective life experience of all researchers as gamers and language learners, we believe introducing this as part of the interview was useful as it can inform readers about the work on videogames taking place in the Global South. The final part (Hurrying Up) collects Gee's closing thoughts as a call to action for education given our current political climate. A closing reflection about the aftermath of our framework after speaking to Jim and some parting thoughts from our researchers bookend this chapter.

2 Blazing the Trail

Raúl A. Mora: *What Video Games Can Teach us about Learning and Literacy* (Gee, 2003) is probably one of the biggest sources for gaming researchers. Most of the chapters in this book cited that book or some of your work.

James Gee:	When you are writing a book like this, being first is very important. You know, I was writing that book with no ties to the gaming field. I had gotten into games by playing with my six-year-old and I was sitting there writing that because I had a passion for it, but I wasn't that connected to the gaming world. When we first went to conferences and stuff, we were alone, there was nothing. People were waiting for someone to say it is a new technology and it has all sorts of promise. I was just lucky and then the book sold of course a lot of copies for that reason.
Mora:	Did you expect the reaction to be as it was?
Gee:	When I had really gotten into playing and I was writing the book, I had fantasies that I would get invited to the game developers conference, I didn't even really know how to function. So eventually, I did get invited to the game developers' conference. A guy named Eric Zimmerman, a very well-known game designer, got up while he was sitting in the audience at the end of my talk and said, "You know, many of the game designers you talk about are people sitting here in the audience, so why don't we just turn around and ask them if your principles are true". I thought, "Well, this is a true defining moment". He turned around and asked Warren Spector, "are these principles in your games?" And he said, "of course they are". I love that story because if he had said no, we wouldn't be talking; it was an amazing moment.
Mora:	Over the past decade the field of gaming research has really grown. Being one of the pioneers in the field, what areas of study do you find have been the most salient?
Gee:	Well, you see, in the beginning, we were trying to start this program. So, I started this program in Wisconsin, on games serving the society, with people like Kurt Squire, my student Constance Steinkuehler, and others. I said, we don't want this to be a typical academic area, where you engage in ludic postmodernism stuff, we wanted to keep this about the impact of the technology and the promise the technology has. I think the most promising part of the field is still those people who want to get real communications between academics who want to study games and the developers who make them so this stays in the world.
Mora:	How do you see this phenomenon of gamers becoming teachers affecting how we view pedagogy and classroom practice?

Gee: I see today young assistant professors who come out of the gamer generation who don't see technology as something special; it's what you do with it that makes it special. They are good at it, but they want to use it to make an impact, not just for publishing. They want big challenges, they want to work with other people.

So, if we got teachers who were tech-savvy in the sense of being able to mod, not just consume, but being able to understand how to make them, how to use them and modify them to get across problem solving, we would transform teaching. That would be more important than using any game at school.

Mora: How do we deal with the skeptics?

Gee: You just have to get out of the mentality that says it's all about shooting, violence and AAA games. You have to say look, this is the technology. It's going to be as powerful in planning class as the book, but it's a different technology, putting people in new worlds to solve problems in new ways and you introduce them to real games that are not just AAA shooters. You're not pushing the games, but the technology of building simulated experiences where a person has a surrogate body and they enter that experience to see the world in a new way and use tools they've never seen and then come out and be able to work with other people, having the attitude to change the world.

3 Unchartered Territories

Mora: I am going to read the questions from my research team. Tyrone argues that gamers and gaming experiences are no longer in a "sandbox" or a safe environment. Now it's online. So, he is wondering about how that may influence gamers who use English as a second language, and how they can really overcome being in this new gaming environment.

Gee: I've talked a lot about what I like to call the g/Game. The game is the soft one, it's what you bought on a disk or downloaded. The Game is the whole social setting around it. It's what you do with other people, going to the interest-driven sites, modding, discussing. When we design experiences for people, we are designing Games and it's, show me your software and show me the sorts of social settings and activities you built around it and how I can leave the game to do stuff, how I can do stuff in the game with other people and how I can do stuff out of the game, bring it back to the game. When we see it as a Game that's part of a larger social setting, new dangers arise. You get mad people, you can have a Nazi game, but that's our responsibility. So, people try to build game settings with these social variables around them for Autistic kids, for ADHD kids, for victims of child abuse. So, their responsibility is to go out there and use these principles to build a game and a social setting that is life-enhancing and safe. If it was easy everyone would be doing it. You can't just focus on the shooters, the AAA stuff.

Mora: Daniel says that one of the problems that we have is that the games are repetitive in terms of communicative scenarios and in-game patterns. So, he is wondering about the effect that those situations can have on second language learners using the games to improve their language skills.

Gee: Gaming for language skills is an interesting topic. I would say there is no other topic that people have come to read more about and tons of people are making games for language learning. But, none of them have really taken hold. I don't know if you have ever seen the game the U.S. Defense Department made on learning Iraqi Arabic. It uses voice recognition, you go in as a soldier but you are with a mentor, and you have to talk to the people and learn Iraqi Arabic but in a culturally-sensitive way. So, it's teaching you the culture and the language while you are embedded in it. It's a very powerful concept, we now have it available in other languages, so there is no doubt it will be a great area.

About repetitiveness, what you want to do is not make people quite aware that they are doing a lot of repetition because they are motivated for a higher goal and they are integrated. Another thing I would love to see with people in the MOBA games and the other platforms like augmented reality is using each other as language teachers. Now we are able to do something, whether we use it to help each other in other languages. You can use the social aspect to make up for the lack of voice recognition. And you can get people doing stuff learning language under the guise of operating with other people, engage in all sorts of language help and language exchange. There will be ways to do language teaching through voice recognition and being embedded in worlds, but also there will be ways to

	do it by networking people socially for a task. Teenagers are doing that, learning each other's languages because they have a shared passion for anime or anything else.
Mora:	I just wanted to share a little bit of our work. What we are doing right now is we are analyzing different genres of videogames, looking at how language, English in this case, becomes a communicative resource for gamers with one very particular purpose, to win the game. We coined a concept and we presented last year at LRA called Language-as-Victory...
Gee:	I love it, I love it.
Mora:	...which refers to the different ways in which gamers, or second language users reach out to the language, depending on the genre and the moment in the game and even in the sense of network, which you talked about earlier, and how that helps them to develop and improve their position in the game, with the ultimate goal of winning or succeeding in the game.
Gee:	I think that's great, it leverages social collaboration and I hope that as you do that as the people using English as a resource they do see images and actions connected to the words not just definitions. To really learn a language, you have to know how it applies to the world. It's like reading a game manual with no game. You know if you read a game manual, it makes no sense if you've never played the game; when you play the game, the game gives meaning to the manual right? Every word the manual has refers to an image or an action or some dialogue in the game. It doesn't refer to a dictionary. So, language learning does require language to get married to action, image, dialogue; and what you are doing should be great for that. You have to start associating [words] with images, action and dialogue. I've got like a power up, I've got to see what they look like, I've got to see what they do if you really want me to remember what it means.
Mora:	I have the final question from Sebastián. He is looking at videogames as storytelling devices, transcending game mechanics and problem-solving to engage with the narratives of videogames as central to both the learning process and the student. So, in that sense, he would like to know, how feasible and how possible, or what is the potential for an analysis of videogame stories in English classrooms along with traditional literature.
Gee:	That's a very good question right now. You know when I first started this and it was just getting going there was a massive

war among designers on whether story should be in a game. That debate is over because almost all modern games including AAA games have very elaborate stories. However, there is a new genre of games now that intrigues me which I call *walk around games*. [where] you walk around and discover. And you do stuff, but the emphasis is on walking around and doing stuff in order to patch the story back together, to live the story. I think that's a very powerful genre. And those are being made in large volumes, there are dozens of them now. In the *Life is Strange* (Dontnod Entertainment, 2015) series where you are a teenager, not only do you enact a story and discover one, but at any time when you make choices you can unravel the choice and see what would have happened had you made another one. So, we have settled the debate about stories in games. And now we are moving on not only to have better stories in commercial games but to make some games' primary motivation to is the story, and there are many of them.

4 Hurrying Up

Mora: From your point of view, as a research community, as a teaching community, as teacher educators, what can we do to help take literacies of play seriously?

Gee: By explicating play in terms of what are the identities we use, what are the skills we use, what are the norms we use, how do we actively modify it. In other words, let's talk about the literacy of play, the literacy of gaming, that is your knowledge of the values, skills, norms, activity, practices, ways of being in the world of a gamer. Ultimately the literacy of gaming is me introducing you to the identity of a gamer, a gamer researcher. So, what we are talking about today is getting people to see themselves as learners in an entirely different way, to see a learner as someone who is proactive, someone who mods and not just consumes, who participates in collective intelligence with others and doesn't do everything with others. You know we are talking about a new type of person. A type of person who engages in collective intelligence, a person who wants to take challenges that are hard, that wants to work with other people to really solve problems and wants to be a lifelong learner and teacher of themselves. That's what we are trying to

Mora: talk about, a modern human being that can change this shitty world we've got and to do that we have to make that identity compelling.

Mora: Our final question for you is: How do you see these ideas we have talked about, and how would they intertwine with issues of educational policy?

Gee: That probably changes from country to country. In America, there is a big debate, should we change our schools in an incremental way, you know make them better but basically keep schooling as the paradigm we know, which is the view of the Gates foundation, or should we completely change the paradigm of schooling? I argue, that just tweaking the model we have, keeping the traditional grammar of schooling, keeping schooling as we have known it for over 150 years is not going to work. We must change the entire paradigm of school.

That means getting people in multiple worlds, virtual, real, collective intelligence, networking multiple technologies to be a producer and maker and not just a consumer, participating with others across the globe in interest driven sites and affinity spaces is passion. You know, leveraging passion for challenge. It's a big task, and we don't have 100 years to do it. You know we just elected a clown as president. An absolute clown. And we have enough nuclear weapons to put the rest of the world completely out of business. So, we should be not afraid and not pessimistic, we should just be in a hurry.

5   Conclusion

We have to admit that interviewing James Paul Gee was thrilling and inspirational. Although Raúl is more aware of his work beyond videogames, for all past and present #TeamLaV researchers, Gee's work on videogames has been influential to construct our homegrown frameworks. Interviewing Gee has inspired us far beyond this chapter. During the second semester of 2018, we drew from this interview to develop an interactive educational experience encompassing all our ongoing research at the Literacies in Second Languages Project, "Doers, Makers, Modders: The Future of Language Education in the Fourth Industrial Revolution". Those three words were the words that Gee used in this interview to describe the future teacher roles. Through our interactive experience, four of our current researchers (Walter Castaño, Carlos Andrés Gaviria, Julián

Londoño-Mazo, and Sebastián Ramírez) shared with high school students what the LaV framework might look in practice through a multimodal experience that approached students to the framework itself through theory and practice.

Beyond this experience, Gee's thoughts about our LaV framework have informed our current research (also including two other researchers, Juan Camilo Mazo and Carlos Sánchez), as we have further expanded our framework as an expanded experience that encompasses, as stated in the introduction, linguistic, semiotic, and aesthetic elements that are part of the entire gaming enterprise. However, Gee's interview also helped us interrogate what the LaV framework means beyond exploring videogames. Our team past and present has included gamers who are hardcore (i.e. extensive game time and active participation in communities), semi-professional (Michael, Juan Camilo, Carlos), or, as in the case of Julián, professional. Looking back at the last section, we realized that their background as gamers who are becoming teachers, rather than a source of conflict, was an opportunity to help transform teaching from within. A major consequence of this interview and our ongoing work has been giving a closer look at the idea of *gamification* (Eusse, 2017). We are revisiting the idea of gamification on two levels: On the one hand, we are looking at how gamification may actually help reshape our entire research design (Mora, Castaño, Gaviria, Londoño-Mazo, Mejía, & Ramírez, 2019), from how we (re)organize ourselves as a team and how we (re)design our research methodology for this project. On the other hand, we want to revisit how our gamer-researchers turned teachers may begin to infuse gaming elements in their practice, a project we have labeled the *LaV Gamification Initiative* (Mora, et al, 2019a, 2019b) and which we intend to share with the world in full in a few years.

We end this chapter with a collective vignette from the younger authors of this chapter, Sebastián, Tyrone, Daniel, and Michael,

> Education is outdated because nowadays there are multiple worlds where the youth feels comfortable enough to indeed, face the challenges they are encouraging and proposing worldwide through videogames, and somehow, they feel passionate about it until the point to, leave everything behind and that is a huge red flag to modern society, there is something that we are doing completely wrong.
>
> We should not be afraid to propose new approaches to knowledge because, currently we are in a hurry to fight against a mighty enemy and we should not be afraid of that at all. We now have a big change to greatly transform the actual teaching paradigm. It will not be an easy quest, but with effort and constant work we feel confident that we can develop those skills and find the perfect equilibrium between gaming and learning.

References

Dontnod Entertainment. (2015). *Life is strange* [Video game]. Yokohama, Japan: Square Enix.

Eusse, E. (2017). Gamification. *LSLP Micro-Papers, 47*. Retrieved from https://www.literaciesinl2project.org/uploads/3/8/9/7/38976989/lslp-micro-paper-47-gamification.pdf

Gaviria, C. A. (2018). Gamers as L2 learners. *LSLP Micro-Papers, 55*. Retrieved from https://www.literaciesinl2project.org/uploads/3/8/9/7/38976989/lslp-micro-paper-55-gamers-as-l2-users.pdf

Gee, J. P. (1999). *An introduction to discourse analysis: Theory and method*. New York, NY: Routledge.

Gee, J. P. (2001). Reading as situated language: A sociocognitive perspective. *Journal of Adolescent & Adult Literacy, 44*(8), 714–725.

Gee, J. P. (2003). *What video games can teach us about learning and literacy*. New York, NY: Palgrave Macmillan.

Gee, J. P. (2008). *Social linguistics and literacies: Ideology in discourses*. New York, NY: Routledge.

Mora, R. A., Castaño, W., Gaviria, C. A., Londoño-Mazo, J., Mazo, J. C., Mejía, S., & Ramírez, S. (2019, May). *Gamifying the research design: #TeamLaV's methodological proposal*. Paper presented at the Fifteenth International Congress of Qualitative Inquiry, University of Illinois, Urbana-Champaign, IL.

Mora, R. A., Castaño, W., Londoño-Mazo, J., Ramírez, S., Mazo, J. C., & Mejía, S. (2019, April). *The translanguaging of gaming literacies: A study of second-language gamers and gaming spaces*. Paper presented at the Annual Meeting of the American Educational Research Association, Toronto.

Mora, R. A., Castaño, S., Hernandez, M., Orrego, T. S., Ramírez, D., & Castaño, W. (2016, December). *Gaming literacies and second languages: When using a second language becomes the key to victory*. Paper presented at the Literacy Research Association 66th Annual Conference, Nashville, TN.

Mora, R. A., Castaño, S., Orrego, T. S., Hernandez, M., & Ramírez, D. (2016). Language-as-victory: A study of gaming literacy practices in second-language contexts. In L. Gómez Chova, A. López Martínez, & I. Candel Torres (Eds.), *INTED2016 Proceedings* (pp. 2823–2831). Valencia, Spain: IATED Academy.

Pope, L. (2014). *Papers, please* [Video game]. 3909 LLC.

PART 2

Playful Explorations

∴

Introduction to Part 2: Playful Explorations

Antero Garcia, Jennifer S. Dail and Shelbie Witte

Though the chapters in this part, too, highlight powerful methodological innovations akin to the work highlighted in the first half of this volume, we center what literacies research *explores, emphasizes,* and *elucidates* within gaming contexts. If games offer the possibility of trying on and exploring worlds previously unseen and unimagined, these chapters peek into some of the ways such opportunities intersect with literacies and learning contexts.

While Engerman's chapter in the first half of this volume hinted at the sociopolitical landscape of videogame culture, Middaugh and Asoto intentionally place their research within the contexts of politics and disagreement within the U.S. today. Bringing together civics and literacies as a rationale for real-world explorations of space and its narratives. Fostering a particular kind of civic innovation (Mirra & Garcia, 2017), this chapter explores what games can reveal for young people about the world around them and their agency within and upon it.

Middaugh and Asoto's examination of civic literacies and the exploration of physical spaces largely untethered from the screens that help mediate videogames is bookended by two chapters that look at very different aspects of participation within "virtual worlds", continuing a line of research in sociology, anthropology, and education (e.g. Boellstorff, 2008; Chen, 2011; Nardi, 2010). Specific to literacies, D'Aveta's and Smith's chapters speak in dialogue with literacies research both within these particular platforms (Dezuanni, 2018; Hollett & Ehret, 2015), and within virtual world exploration writ large (Garcia & Niemeyer, 2017).

D'Aveta's chapter brings together mapmaking, literature, collaboration, and learning within the Minecraft gaming platform. It is a complex assemblage and—at its heart—it speaks to the possibilities of multimodal *writing* within gaming practices. Bringing together exploration of imaginary worlds (on printed pages and digital screens) with a genre of writing that intentionally seeks to define and place boundaries on "space" (e.g. Massey, 2005), this chapter offers a glimpse a particular kind of literacy practice existing at and scribing the boundaries of play.

While D'Aveta traces literacies that build around and across virtual worlds, Mortimore-Smith's contribution explores *within* not only a particular virtual world but within a guild of assembled players, their avatars, and the learning practices they engage in within this instantiation of participatory culture

(Jenkins et al., 2009). Concluding the chapter, Mortimore-Smith importantly calls for "prioritizing playful learning methodologies and fostering a participatory culture within our own classrooms is crucial for achieving meaningful progress" (p. 107).

Considering the infinite worlds to be read and written, explored and imagined, shared and curated for others, the chapters in the second half of this volume take up a playful process of looking and experiencing in the "real" and "virtual" worlds that young people interact. They invite readers to consider the playscape from which new narratives, new literacies, and new playful identities can be studied and designed.

References

Boellstorff, T. (2008). *Coming of age in second life: An anthropologist explores the virtually human.* Princeton, NJ: Princeton University Press.

Chen, M. (2011). *Leet noobs: The life and death of an expert player group in World of Warcraft.* New York, NY: Peter Lang.

Dezuanni, M. (2018). Minecraft and children's digital making: Implications for media literacy education. *Learning, Media and Technology, 43*(3), 236–249.

Garcia, A., & Niemeyer, G. (Eds.). (2017). *Virtual, visible, and viable: Alternate reality games and the cusp of digital gameplay.* New York, NY: Bloomsbury.

Hollett, T., & Ehret, C. (2015). "Bean's world": (Mine) crafting affective atmospheres of gameplay, learning, and care in a children's hospital. *New Media & Society, 17*(11), 1849–1866.

Jenkins, H., Clinton, K., Purushotma, R., Robison, A. J., & Weigel, M. (2009). *Confronting the challenges of participatory culture: Media education for the 21st century.* Chicago, IL: MacArthur Foundation.

Massey, D. (2005). *For space.* London: Sage.

Mirra, N., & Garcia, A. (2017). Re-imagining civic participation: Youth interrogating and innovating in the multimodal public sphere. *Review of Research in Education, 41,* 136–158.

Nardi, B. (2010). *My life as a night elf priest: An anthropological account of World of Warcraft.* Ann Arbor, MI: University of Michigan Press.

CHAPTER 5

Building Civic Literacy in the English Language Arts through Geospatial Play

Ellen Middaugh and Jolynn A. Asato

1   Overarching Questions

1. Why should English Language Arts teachers take on the goals of civic education?
2. How can we motivate youth to be excited about political engagement when politicians do not speak to them?
3. How can *play*, and in particular, *geospatial play*, help youth connect to their communities while learning academic skills?

2   Introduction

As we write this chapter, the dominant tone in news about the U.S. political system and democracy is generally negative. Regardless of political orientation, many voters express a lack of trust and enthusiasm for elected officials and institutions (Gallup, 2016), a trend that is pronounced among youth (Circle, 2016). As a system we find ourselves in a catch-22. On one hand, many youth find political engagement unappealing, because the candidates and discourse are disconnected and unrelatable (Circle, 2016). On the other hand, making politics relevant and engaging requires youth participation in the political system.

The reality is that voting is only empowering when the issues candidates discuss reflect the concerns of the voter. For that to happen, citizens need to be vocal and active in public discourse between elections in order to learn about issues that impact them and raise their concerns to elected officials. These practices make up what Barber (1984) describes as "participatory politics" and which scholars more recently have suggested digital media enable by giving citizens more access to tools to find and share information, engage in dialogue with others, and mobilize resources (Cohen et al., 2012; Soep, 2014). Educators throughout the K-16 system can contribute to the goal of youth civic engagement by helping youth gain the skills and interests that will allow them to participate productively in public discourse.

Preparing and motivating young people to take the leap from seeing a set of unappealing options for engagement to envisioning (and creating) an alternative future in which their voices and needs are at the center of political life requires more than a semester of U.S. Government. It requires multiple opportunities for young people to develop the skills of critical inquiry and analysis of social issues, a sense of agency or internal efficacy that they have or can develop the skills needed for effective civic and political action, a capacity for debate and discussion needed for collective action, and the writing and presentation skills needed for public voice (Gibson & Levine, 2003; Kahne & Middaugh, 2008; Kahne, Middaugh, & Allen, 2015). Perhaps even more importantly, it requires imagination (Evans, 2015)—opportunities to think outside the box from what is, to what ought to be and what could be. Thus, in this chapter, we focus on the intersection of play (opportunities for imagination) and education (opportunities to build skills and attitudes described above) as a space to develop civic literacy with special attention to the question of how technological tools can help enhance this process.

Specifically, we consider how high school English Language Arts courses can more explicitly foster students' civic literacy and how the integration of geospatial play (play that blends the use of geospatial technology such as GPS/mapping technology with exploration of physical space) can support the connection of ELA to Civic Education by taking the practice of literacy development into physical and virtual spaces. First, we describe the connection between civic learning goals and the priorities (articulated in the Common Core) of ELA courses. Next, we describe how geospatial play has been used in educational settings to support those goals. Then, we discuss the potential and limitations of using popular and available games (like Pokemon Go) vs. DIY approaches. We conclude with a discussion of how current models of geospatial play create an intriguing launching point and context for the development of civic literacies, but stops short (without teacher mediation) of creating opportunities for true public voice. This is followed by recommendations for bridging this gap.

3 Civic Education in the English Language Arts Classroom: Converging Priorities

While teachers of all subjects embrace the goals of teaching for citizenship and social justice (Watt et al., 2012), explicit attention to civic education is typically relegated to U.S. Government courses and units. To counter this trend and expand opportunities from civic education throughout the secondary curriculum, scholars have worked with humanities teachers to identify areas where the goals of Civic Education and the Common Core explicitly align and lessons (see Kahne et al., 2018; Middaugh, 2015, and eddaoakland.org for more information).

One area where teachers have been able to advance civic and ELA goals is through units investigating civic issues in order to enhance *research skills* (Common Core Anchor Standards W7, 8, 9), including the ability to find, assess the credibility of and synthesize information. Another approach has been through *academic discussion* (Common Core Anchor Standards SL1) centered around controversial issues that are raised through literature or research. The ability to exchange ideas about a topic using academic language and evidence is both a critical academic skill and an important civic skill (Hess, 2009; Hess & McAvoy, 2014). Finally, ELA teachers have found that encouraging students to exercise *public voice* by calling attention to information about social issues can be a motivating opportunity to practice presentation and communication skills (Common Core Anchor Standards W8, 9; SL 6). The ability to find and assess information about issues of public concern, to debate and discuss such issues with those who may disagree and to express public voice are critical components of empowered citizenship (Kahne, Middaugh, & Allen, 2015; Kahne, Hodgin, & Eidman-Aahdal, 2016), and ELA teachers can play a powerful role in supporting these goals by integrating civic topics into the curriculum while teaching research skills, academic discussion and presentation and communication skills.

Additionally, ELA classrooms are an exciting venue for enhancing civic development because of the power for literature to enhance democratic dispositions, such as empathy (Mirra, 2018) or critical consciousness (Diemer & Rapa, 2016; Watts, Diemer, & Voight, 2011). Citizenship is not just a matter of knowledge and skill but also involves civic commitment or a persistent motivation to contribute to democratic life (Kahne & Sporte, 2009; Youniss & Yates, 1997).

Youniss and Yates (1997) demonstrated through research on service learning how direct experiences with others in the community can foster feelings of *empathy* for their needs and, in turn, a sense of civic commitment. Scholars from the humanities have shown how literary and historical analysis can also support this goal. For example, Endacott and Brooks (2013) suggested that teachers can foster historical empathy (a combination of historical and affective engagement) by having students draw connections (similarities and differences) to historical figures they learn about through text while at the same time drawing attention to historical context and why context matters. Situating their cognitive and emotional analysis in the historical context is believed to be key to preventing simplistic conclusions of superiority (Endacott & Brooks, 2013), dispositions that are useful for civic engagement with a diverse population.

An experimental study by Kidd and Castano (2013) found that reading literary fiction enhanced Theory of Mind (the ability to understand that others hold different perspectives and have different emotional states) providing support for the contention that literature can support civic dispositions. Indeed, Mirra (2018) has recently argued in a book-length treatment for the potential of ELA classrooms as venues for fostering "critical civic empathy" (p. 7).

Another way of discussing democratic dispositions is through development of "critical consciousness", defined as a combination of sociopolitical critique combined with a sense of agency (Watts, Diemer, & Voight, 2011, p. 43; Diemer & Rapa, 2016). Civic education in this tradition education teaches young people to be the *authors* of civic engagement—identifying and framing issues and suggesting action—not just participants in civic action defined by others (Ginwright & Cammarota, 2006; Kirshner, 2015).

The potential of ELA classes to support the development critical consciousness has been well articulated in transactional and critical theories of literacy (Damico, Campano, & Carste, 2009). When students read texts not just for understanding of what is being communicated, but with an eye to the assumptions, priorities, and agenda of the writer, they become active participants in the construction of meaning. Freebody and Luke's (1990) Four Resources Model of Literacy Instruction suggests when students engage with text (novels, videos, etc.), they should not only have opportunities to decode the text, but to use text as a means for thinking about their own circumstances and to actively analyze texts for the author's attentions, assumptions and omissions. This type of analysis not only helps for identifying bias, but also gives the reader insight into how narratives shape meaning for others, privileging some interpretations and perspectives over others.

Taking this further, many media scholars advocate putting students in the role of "text maker" where they can remix and re-author narratives, bringing their experiences to the forefront (Lankshear & Knobel, 2003). This type of capacity to tell stories that reframe narratives has been a critical resource for youth on the margins, as in the example of the DREAM activists who took a dominant narrative of dangerous and illegal aliens and retold their stories in many ways, through pop culture and political activism to change the narrative (Gamber-Thompson & Zimmerman, 2016).

When thinking about the shared goals of civic education and ELA to enhance research skills, evidence-based discussion about controversial issues, communication and presentation skills, empathy and critical consciousness, we must also consider that these practices are increasingly taking place online and using digital tools. Just as the internet provides access to a wide array of information, perspectives and audiences, it also places great demands on individuals to find and assess the credibility of information (Kahne, Bowyer, & Middaugh, 2015; Kahne & Bowyer, 2016; Journell, 2019), to successfully navigate sometimes harsh differences of opinion (Middaugh, Bowyer, & Kahne, 2016) and to get the attention of a wide but often indifferent audience (Levine, 2008). We are seeing emerging evidence that students need opportunities to practice these skills using the technology and within the contexts that they will be operating as citizens (Clark & Marchi, 2017; Kahne, Hodgin, & Eidman-Aahdahl, 2016; Middaugh, 2018; Middaugh & Evans, 2018).

Research to date has created insights into how we can prepare youth to use the internet and social media to their advantage as citizens. As we will discuss below, geospatial play can take advantage of these gains and provide interesting curricular opportunities. However, as virtual and augmented reality rapidly advance, we have little understanding of what it means for youth civic engagement. Such technologies can provide new mechanisms for telling stories and inspire empathy, but these tools are often developed for youth as consumers to be led. Thus, as we discuss below, we also explore how geospatial play can be leveraged to provide opportunities for students to not only be critical consumers of media but to see in themselves the capacity for authorship of many kinds of text, supporting the goals of critical consciousness.

4 Geospatial Play as a Context for Learning

Geospatial play provides an intriguing opportunity to blend the advantages of video game play and civic education. Geospatial play can take many forms, but typically involves participants moving through the physical world (museums, parks, city) to accomplish a goal (Garcia & Middaugh, 2015). While geospatial play, in the form of the old-fashioned treasure hunt, has always existed, the addition of mobile technology, the internet, graphic design, and augmented reality have expanded the possibilities. Players may be local or stretch across great distances, data can be mapped, and the physical world can be manipulated with the use of virtual reality.

Geospatial play shares the core elements of games—goals, rules, a feedback system, and voluntary action—identified by McGonagal (2010) as features of games in general and videogames in particular that may encourage cognitive, behavioral and affective engagement (Deater-Deckard et al., 2013) and thus make them useful contexts for learning. Educational videogames such as iCivics (which leads players through mock elections, application of immigration policy, etc.) have been shown to promote knowledge of civic facts and processes (Blevin, LeCompte, & Wells, 2014). However, as Stoddard et al. (2016) note, the closed game world, which allows for effective delivery of content, also presents potential concerns about oversimplification of complex civic issues, requiring teachers to play a bridging role. Middaugh (2016) extends this critique analyzing the social and emotional components of civic engagement, noting the importance of civic education to not only provide understandings of the structure and function of government, but to provide opportunities to develop empathy, productively channel political anger, and to imagine alternative arrangements.

Since the dawn of the micro-computer, educators have sought to use technology to enhance play and learning. Griffin and Cole (1984) used computer assisted play activities to demonstrate how a combination of fantasy world, peer interaction, and adult scaffolding can combine to support learning. Most notably in Cole's work was the observation that play can provide important opportunities for students who may be disengaged or marginalized from traditional classrooms. In a play context, students are encouraged to break out of their well-established classroom roles and imagine themselves as participants in the game. Content to which they are resistant can be reintroduced as game activities. They can be encouraged to imagine themselves as scientists, activists, literary or historical figures. At its best, play provides opportunities to experiment with ideas, reimagine identities, and for the player to not only consume information and interact with others, but to take on the role of content producer and author. Players are not only consuming information, interacting with peers, but acting as authors.

Our interest in geospatial play builds on the potential of video games and play, but provides two elements that we think are relevant for civic learning opportunities. First, geospatial play situates the game content in the physical world, and thus may provide more meaningful learning than computer-simulated environments (deSouza e Silva & Delacruz, 2006). As players move around the physical world, they engage with multiple literacies engaging with images, words, sights and sounds, supporting active participation in the game, and with the right scaffolding, can serve as a bridge for students become authors in the narratives they are studying (fictional, historical, civic, etc.) However, to be an author one needs an audience (Levine, 2008). Our second feature of geospatial play supports this goal, as geospatial play commonly requires collaboration and participation in a community, providing opportunities to not only build collaborative skills, but an audience for their ideas. Several scholars have noted the potential of gaming communities as "interest driven" spaces

(Ito et al., 2009) joining a game world provides access to a community and audience in an informal (aka interest driven) space. Third, a unique affordance of geospatial play is that the players are generating data and often have access to that data. GPS technology provides players with data as they move throughout space—distance traveled, duration of travel, current and average speed—and when this data is logged and combined with the data of other players, it becomes social science data that can be analyzed (Christie, 2007).

On a final note, while integration of geospatial play into the curriculum still requires significant adaptation and teacher mediation, the game mechanics of many games that support geospatial play are relatively simple, removing one layer of barriers for teacher (and students) who may not be avid gamers. Advocates of using geospatial technology in classrooms point to their flexibility as "multi-disciplinary, inquiry-driven, field-based tools" that can be integrated across the curricula (Christie, 2007).

5 Geospatial Play: Practical Adaptations

As with videogames, examples of geospatial play and learning vary from using popular existing games as platforms for learning (for example Pokemon Go, Ingress and Geocaching) to using specially designed platforms created in universities for specific purposes to educators and students themselves design games. In what follows, we describe existing examples of how geospatial play has been integrated into the classroom and draw connections to the opportunities for research, dialogue and public voice as well as empathy and authorship. These uses are not mutually exclusive, but give educators some practical examples to build from. We then conclude with some analysis of the advantages and disadvantages of using existing games vs. designing games for these purposes.

5.1 *Treasure Hunt*

Perhaps the most straightforward application of geospatial play in educational settings is the treasure hunt, where the purpose of the game is to find and mark resources in their classroom, school, community and beyond. This approach to motivating exploration of resources has existed long before existence of GPS and mobile technology. Educators often use passports, asset maps and photography to encourage students to explore their community and consciously connect classroom content to their daily lives. In civic education, the asset map is a common springboard for analyzing resources and needs in the community, which may be followed by a civic action project to address an unmet need or maintain a valuable resource. In math, the treasure hunt may involve finding and taking pictures of shapes in the community. In history, it may be finding historical landmarks.

With geospatial technology, the treasure hunt is enriched as the game can be persistent and social. For example, students reading the novel *Divergent* might engage in a treasure hunt that involves searching for places in the community that represent one of the four virtues represented by the communities in the book—honesty, bravery, intelligence, or kindness/acceptance. When one student finds an example of each and writes about or presents on it, they become participants in the text at an individual level. When 30 students place trackable devices (bugs or QR codes) in each place they identify that represents a virtue, you create a community level representation that can help students connect their individual experiences to community. They may identify places that serve as important sources of support common to all of them and it may open up analysis of differences of experiences—why are some locations places of kindness and acceptance to some but not to others? By adding their analysis and recreating the divisions in the book in the local communities, students engage in literature through personal comparison but also participate in authorship, using the themes of the book to describe their own experience. By surfacing differences among classmates, they apply a critical lens. Additionally, this creates an entry point for connecting personal experiences to shared social experiences, a common entry point for civic education.

5.2 *Dialogue through Data*

Another affordance of geospatial play is the potential to leverage the game for civic dialogue. In the previous example, we note the treasure hunt as a springboard for students to exchange ideas. Other research on digital media and civic dialogue has focused on the ways in which online communities can bring people together across geographical distance and expose them to diverse perspectives. It has been found that youth participation in interest-driven communities organized around hobbies is associated with exposure to diverse perspectives (Kahne, Middaugh, Lee, & Feezell, 2012). Steinkuhler and Williams (2006) also suggest that the kinds of dialogue and collaboration that take place in online gaming worlds plant the seeds of civic engagement as participants work together to resolve conflicts and coordinate action.

In a previous study one of the authors examined the potential of Geocaching as a mechanism for engaging youth in civic dialogue (Garcia & Middaugh, 2015). The GlobalKids Online Leadership program sought to leverage the existence of a large-scale online community associated with geocaching, combined with the integration of play into geographic exploration, to see if youth could use geocaching as an opportunity to initiate dialogue about electoral issues during the 2012 election. Youth worked in teams to research issues that would be impacted by the election (net neutrality, marijuana legalization, etc.), planted the geocaches in their local community with an explanation for those who discovered the caches to move them toward Washington DC if they agree with the issue and away if they disagree. The simple movement of the geocaches served as a form of dialogue with students able to track the overall feelings about these issues as geocachers vote with their feet. Additionally, the online community where people could add comments and share their perspectives on the topics.

5.3 Analysis of Tracking Data

In the example of Race to the WhiteHouse, students analyzed tracking data by seeing where around the globe their geocaches moved, giving them information about how people in the community feel about the issues represented in their caches. This is but one use of analysis of tracking data leveraged by educators. For example, Matya et al. (2008) experimented with engaging university students in a game called CityExplorer, in which players were asked to fill a grid-like representation of their city with markers of resources within the city—libraries, public transportation, etc. accompanied by pictures and descriptions. This exercise creates data about the local city and resources, which can be analyzed dynamically—how far away are certain resources from each other, for example. Other uses of tracking data have included tracking how far a person travels between locations, time taken to complete that travel, availability of wi-fi (and places where wi-fi gaps exist, etc.).

For students who are exploring their communities, these data can be quite valuable civic information. A common research paper among students in high schools in urban areas may include, for example, research on food deserts. Using geospatial technology to create some understanding of where fruits and vegetables can be found in their local community (and perhaps how long each member of the class must travel to between their home and these resources), can provide an illustration of who is impacted by the issue and what it means in real life terms (aka travel time). Using mapping apps to track safe routes home for teens who live in violent neighborhoods can provide an illustration of the impact of neighborhood violence on day-to-day life. Learning to present information through dynamic visual presentation is an increasingly important literacy in the modern work world. Engaging students in geospatial play can give practice with presentation and analysis.

5.4 *Augmented Reality as Empathy Motivator*

One of the most recent developments in considering the role of geospatial play in learning is the question of whether the integration of augmented reality can enhance the game experience in ways that make them more realistic and/or more engaging. Recently, augmented reality games have been used to create experiences that develop prosocial feelings, which lab experiments show to result in later prosocial behavior (Rosenberg, Baughman, & Bailenson, 2013). Educational non-profits like Global Nomads have developed Virtual Reality programs (that can be used in the classroom with smart-phones and a simple cardboard head-set) to augment their global learning curriculum and allow students to immerse themselves in the day-to-day life of other cultures. These relatively non-mobile examples help to demonstrate the educational potential of *virtual* reality.

However, the challenge of virtual reality for geospatial learning lies in the completeness of the immersion, which presents physical dangers if players begin to move around. Thus in geospatial play, the question is how to take advantage of the use of sight, sound and image along with an experience of exploration without creating danger. Augmented reality, which blends some overlay of digital media with experience is where many in the commercial sphere (as we will discuss below with PokemonGo and Ingress) have sought to find the opportunity to blend the immersion of video game play with the physical exploration of geospatial play.

Sakr, Jewitt, and Price (2016) studied a history curriculum that blends aspects of geospatial play and augmented reality. As in geospatial play, students were given a set of tasks to explore a local area where historical events related to WWII took place. The map included a set of markers which students navigated to, and up on exploration of the locations, added their own data. However, to enhance emotional engagement with the topic and invoke historical empathy, the educator-designers augmented the map with images, sound, and video to help students engage with the physical space and historical content. The entire design amounted to creating maps and uploading media to accompany those maps using Evernote (e.g. widely used, affordable, and commercially available technology). Embedded media helped students envision the experience and imagine the sights and sounds of the people living through the experience. Creating their own media using recording and video that captured their understanding of the experience (for example reflections of their reactions to what they are learning "I feel sorry for them" or "I would be scared" images they create "in tribute") allows students to participate as authors in the historical narrative.

5.5 *Placing Students in the Community: Geospatial Play and Authorship*

A final way that educators can leverage geospatial play for learning is as a means for inviting students to create narratives and tell stories. When blended with exploration of community, this can become a mechanism for civic expression. For example, educators have described how students' exploration of community, combined with mapping their travels (for example using Map my Walk App) and taking pictures and screen-shots of their locations, can be used as a jumping off point for creating narrative, such as "Welcome to my Neighborhood" (Smith, 2016). Similarly, a recent education blog suggests that Pokemon Go can support critical literacies begins with the potential of the game to encourage neighborhood exploration, but with the next step, taking note of surrounding location and asking questions like, "What kind of world does Squirtle live in?" as an impetus for analysis of local environment (Heik, 2016). Using the fantasy world as an invitation to simply not recreate, but perhaps speculate and use imagination (What kind of world *could* Squirtle live in?) invites students to think through alternatives to existing problems in their local neighborhoods, something Evans (2015) describes as "digital civic imagination". In this use of geospatial play, the game play serves as an impetus for neighborhood exploration, the teacher scaffolding of providing critical questions creates opportunities for analysis using the media collected during play, and the integration of that media (maps and pictures and recordings) into the final product provides opportunities for creative communication. Students learn to use different forms of media to author their own narratives about their communities and the issues that matter.

Another way of thinking about using geospatial play to develop authorship is in the act of game creation. Those who design games inspire action on the part of their players—whether the action is pressing buttons to feed fish, plan trajectories to launch birds, or, in the case of Global Kids game, "NYC Haunts" to use geospatial play to solve the mystery of the social, economic or environmental conditions that led to the demise of an historical character. In this case, students use their knowledge to author a game and gain the attention of their audience (the players). To support processes like these, the MIT Scheller Teacher Education Program (STEP) lab has created a game design app called "Taleblazer" which creates a basic platform that can be adapted for teachers and/or students to create mobile games aligned with different kinds of content. In this version, the players are the audience and the game is the narrative.

6 Joining an Existing Game Community Versus Design It Yourself

In the examples above, we demonstrate some of the uses of geospatial play to further the shared goals of civic education and the humanities to foster skills of research, discussion and public voice as well as to encourage empathy and critical consciousness. The examples shared draw on a mixture of leveraging (a) existing gaming communities developed by others, sometimes for commercial purposes, (b) specially developed games or apps created by universities, and (c) cheap and commercially available software for educators and/or students to design their own games.

Each of these approaches offers advantages and disadvantages. Currently, the three most popular existing communities for geospatial play including Geocaching, Ingress and Pokemon Go. What all three of these games offer is an existing community of players, a platform to connect players that is maintained by experts, and some form of moderation of the community. To the extent that a game is popular, this offers educators a big advantage in reducing the amount of time needed to teach the basics of game play. This is perhaps one reason for a flurry of blogs with titles like, "Pokemon Go: What education should be" (Gracey, 2017) as the game gained widespread popularity within weeks of its release. Any teacher hoping to use geospatial play in their classroom in September 2016 could likely count on at least a subset of their students having familiarity with the game.

Furthermore, each of these games has some design element that makes it attractive to players. Geocaching uses tracking devices to allow players to leave and discover unexpected items in unexpected locations (every day sites or out in nature). With Ingress and Pokemon Go, both use augmented reality so that through phones, players "discover" portals (Ingress) or characters (Pokemon). These features create elements of surprise and signal the transformation of regular walk or street corner into activities and sites of play. Additionally, to the extent that games are popular, there is an existing community for players to interact with. When trying to reach a wide spread community for the purposes of civic dialogue or to have an audience for public voice, a popular game can have advantages. If the game is moderated and has some norms of engagement, concerns about civility or productive dialogue and ameliorated.

On the other hand, the use of existing games come with limitations. The communities that come with the games may be fleeting (the first round of boom and bust of Pokemon Go has taken less than a year) or niche (geocaching while popular among nature enthusiasts and Boy Scouts may not feel like a familiar or welcoming community to all). Because the games are designed and moderated by others, the opportunities for authorship and customization are limited and when present have to be run through moderators. Finally, the features that make Pokemon Go so appealing—cool characters and a well-developed game world—may also compete with rather than augment educational goals. While one *can* certainly take note of a community resource or historical location while hunting and battling Pokemon, that activity is certainly not as engaging. One has to question whether students would be more interested in taking such notes if they were simply sent out with that goal than if it was an activity that distracts from the gaming goal. This is not to discourage from use of existing games but rather to evaluate the goals of geospatial play alongside the affordances of the existing game and engage in some trouble-shooting.

At the other extreme, educators (with their students) can use smart phones or tablets along with commercially available but relatively affordable apps (mapping and productivity) for geospatial learning (use of geospatial technology to achieve learning goals) or to create geospatial play. Recalling McGonagal's (2010) discussion of the basic features of videogame play—goals, rules, a feedback system, and voluntary action—when activities integrate these features (for example NYC Haunts), they take advantage of the elements of game play that make learning engaging. This clearly puts a greater burden on educators. Even when the technology aspect is simple, the idea of creating games and opportunities for play is not often encouraged in secondary education—either on the part of teachers or students. Additionally, while the DIY version gives greater opportunities for authorship, what it does not provides as easily is an audience or a community for dialogue. Finding someone to play the game is not always easy.

This is where educator networks become important. University sponsored games like Tale Blazers can solve some of the problems of creating a "game" infrastructure for teachers to build off of. However, creating a persistent community around a game is a broader challenge. Within the world of youth media production and blogging, networks of teachers are beginning to solve the audience problem. Examples such as YouthVoices Live and Out of Eden are spaces where classrooms join a network that is moderated and education focused. While not as organic as user generated spaces, what is provided here is an opportunity for audience. When students in one classroom post content, they can call on the community to react and provide commentary. Educator-generated versions of geospatial play would also benefit from such networks. When games are created in one classroom, players can be recruited in other locations.

In a different vein, the question of reaching an audience and recruiting players can also be incorporated into the activity. Increasingly in the work-force, games are used to spread advertising, collect data from users, and convey information. Inviting students to analyze existing uses of games and to take on the question of how to recruit players into their games, can help build these skills while developing critical media literacy skills.

7   Conclusion: Translating Exploration, Dialogue, and Authorship into Public Voice

The examples we describe throughout this chapter illustrate the many ways in which the goals of the humanities and civic education align, and when combined with geospatial play, can motivate young people to explore and act as authors of their civic lives drawing using technology and media. Best practice in civic education often involves opportunities for students to explore their communities, map assets and identify gaps and share similarities and differences in perspective with others (Gibson & Levine, 2003). Analyzing existing narratives and creating their own narratives is an important step towards critical consciousness as it gives students a productive answer to the challenge of what to do when they discover injustices or problems that may otherwise lead to cynicism or apathy. However, a key point of tension between the goals of civic education and history/ELA lies in the importance of taking action. Within civic education, this is often seen as a critical step that lies between students simply becoming discouraged by the analysis of social issues and becoming motivated to be part of public life (Diemer & Rapa, 2016).

When students become the authors of narratives about their local conditions and issues that matter to them *and* "go public" with those narratives to raise awareness and inspire or invite others into action, these purposes are bridged. Youth need an audience if the creation of narrative is going to be empowering. Whether it is a small audience of like-minded peers (critical to building community and movements) or a larger audience of people they want to persuade or ask to take some action. The "audience problem" (Levine, 2008) should not be dismissed when considering the potential for authorship to turn into public voice. Currently, geospatial play provides a useful jumping off point for inviting students into exploration and authorship (important steps). However, the power is considerably enhanced when we explicitly address the question of audience. This step is all too frequently overlooked in civic education (where the question of audience is seen a secondary to motivation) and in digital media and learning (where the audience is often assumed), but is one that we need to take seriously if we want to see young people translate the skills and dispositions they develop in school into long term commitment to public life.

References

Barber, B. (1984). *Strong democracy: Participatory politics for a new age.* Berkeley, CA: University of California Press.

Bowyer, B., Kahne, J., & Middaugh, E. (2015). Youth comprehension of political messages in YouTube videos. *New Media and Society* (Advance online publication). doi:10.1177/1461444815611593

Christie, A. (2007, Winter). Using GPS and geocaching engages, empowers and enlightens middle school teachers and students. *Meridian: A Middle School Computer Technologies Journal, 10*(1).

CIRCLE. (2016). *Millennial poll analysis: An in-depth look at youth attitudes, tendencies, and ideology.* Retrieved March 19, 2017, from http://civicyouth.org/wp-content/uploads/2016/10/2016-Millennial-Poll-Analysis.pdf

Clark, L. S., & Marchi, R. (2017). *Young people and the future of news: Social media and the rise of connective journalism.* New York, NY: Cambridge University Press.

Cohen, C. J., Kahne, J., Bowyer, B., Middaugh E., & Rogowski, J. (2012). *Participatory politics: New media and youth political action.* Oakland, CA: Youth and Participatory Politics Research Network.

Damico, J., Campano, G., & Harste, J. (2009). Transactional theory and critical theory in reading comprehension. In S. Israel & G. Duffy (Eds.), *Handbook of research on reading comprehension.* New York, NY: Routledge.

Deater-Deckard, K., Chang, M., & Evans, M. (2013). Engagement states and learning from educational games. *New Directions for Child Development, 139,* 21–30.

de Souza e Silva, A., & Delacruz, G. C. (2006). Hybrid reality games reframed: Potential uses in educational contexts. *Games and Culture, 1*(3), 231–251.

Diemer, M., & Rapa, L. (2016). Unraveling the complexity of critical consciousness, political efficacy, and political action among marginalized adolescents. *Child Development, 87*(1) 221–238.

Endacott, J., & Brooks, S. (2013). An updated theoretical and practical model for promoting historical empathy, *Social Studies Research & Practice, 8*(1), 41–58. Retrieved March 25, 2017, from http://www.socstrpr.org/wp-content/uploads/2013/04/MS_06482_no3.pdf

Evans, C. (2015). The nuts and bolts of digital civic imagination [Blog post]. DML Central. Retrieved March 25, 2017, from https://dmlcentral.net/the-nuts-and-bolts-of-digital-civic-imagination/

Freebody, P., & Luke, A. (1990). "Literacies" programs: Debates and demands in cultural context. *Prospect, 5,* 7–15.

Gallup. (2016). *Trust in government.* Retrieved from http://www.gallup.com/poll/5392/trust-government.aspx

Gamber-Thompson, L., & Zimmerman, A. (2016). DREAMing citizenship: Undocumented youth, coming out, and pathways to participation. In H. Jenkins, S. Shrestove, L. Gamber-Thompson, N. Kligler-Vilenchik, & A.M. Zimmerman (Eds.), *By any media necessary*. New York, NY: New York University Press.

Garcia, A., & Middaugh, E. (2015). Lost, sweaty and engaged in dialogue: The civic opportunities of geospatial play. In B. Kirshner & E. Middaugh (Eds.), *#youthaction: Becoming political in the digital age*. Charlotte, NC: Information Age Publishing.

Gibson, C., & Levine, P. (2003). *The civic mission of schools*. New York, NY & Washington, DC: The Carnegie Corporation of New York and the Center for Information and Research on Civic Learning.

Gracey, L. (2017). *Pokemon go: What education should be. Technotes*. Retrieved from https://blog.tcea.org/pokemon-go/

Griffin, P., & Cole, M. (1984). Current activity for the future: The zo-ped. In B. Rogoff & J. V. Wertsch (Eds.), *Children's learning in the zone of proximal development* (New Directions for Child Development, Vol. 23). San Francisco, CA: Jossey-Bass.

Heik, T. (2016). 5 ways to use Pokemon Go for critical learning [Blog post]. Teach for Thought. Retrieved March 25, 2017 from http://www.teachthought.com/the-future-of-learning/technology/5-ways-to-use-pokemon-go-for-critical-learning/

Hess, D. E. (2009). *Controversy in the classroom: The democratic power of discussion* (Kindle ed.). New York, NY: Taylor & Francis.

Hess, D. E., & McAvoy, P. (2014). *The political classroom: Evidence and ethics in democratic education*. New York, NY: Routledge.

Ito, M., Baumer, S., Bittanti, M., Boyd, D., Cody, R., Herr-Stephenson, B., ... Lange, P. C. (2010). *Hanging out, messing around, and geeking out: Kids living and learning with new media*. Cambridge, MA: MIT Press.

Kahne, J., & Bowyer, B. (2016). Educating for democracy in a partisan age: Confronting the challenges of motivated reasoning and misinformation. *AERJ, 54*(1), 3–34. doi:10.3102/0002831216679817

Kahne, J., Hodgin, E., & Eidman-Aahdahl, E. (2016). Redesigning civic education for the digital age: Participatory politics and the pursuit of democratic engagement. *Theory & Research in Social Education, 44*(1), 1–35.

Kahne, J., Hodgin, E., Evans, C., & Choi, Y. W. (2018). Expanding the opportunity structure for civic education in the digital age: A strategy for reform. In W. G. Tierney, Z. B. Corwin, & A. Ochsner (Eds.), *Diversifying digital learning: Online literacy and educational opportunity*. Baltimore, MD: Johns Hopkins University Press.

Kahne, J., & Middaugh, E. (2008). High quality civic education: What is it and who gets it? *Social Education, 72*(1), 34–39.

Kahne, J., Middaugh, E., & Allen, D. (2015). Youth, new media and the rise of participatory politics. In D. Allen & J. Light (Eds.), *Youth, new media and citizenship*. Chicago, IL: University of Chicago Press.

Kahne, J., Middaugh, E., Lee, N. J., & Feezell, J. T. (2012). Youth online activity and exposure to diverse perspectives. *New Media & Society, 14,* 492. doi:10.1177/1461444811420271

Kahne, J. E., & Sporte, S. E. (2008). Developing citizens: The impact of civic learning opportunities on students' commitment to civic participation. *American Educational Research Journal, 45*(3), 738–766.

Kidd, D., & Castano, E. (2013). Reading literary fiction improves theory of mind. *Science, 342*(6156), 377–380. doi:10.1126/science.1239918

Lankshear, C., & Knobel, M. (2003). *New literacies changing knowledge and classroom learning.* Philadelphia, PA: Open University Press.

Levine, P. (2008). A public voice for youth: The audience problem in digital media and civic education. In W. Lance Bennett (Ed.), *Civic life online: Learning how digital media can engage youth* (pp. 119–138). Cambridge, MA: MIT Press.

Matyas, S., Matyas, C., Schlieder, C., Kiefer, P., Mitari, H., & Kamata, M. (2008). Designing location-based mobile games with a purpose: Collecting geospatial data with CityExplorer. In *ACE '08 Proceedings of the 2008 International Conference on Advances in Computer Entertainment Technology* (pp. 244–247). Retrieved March 19, 2017, from http://dl.acm.org/citation.cfm?id=1501806

McGonagal, J. (2011). *Reality is broken, why games make us better and how they can change the world.* New York, NY: Penguin.

Middaugh, E. (2015). *Digital civic literacy in Oakland high schools* (EDDA Research Brief No. 2). Retrieved March 25, 2017, from http://eddaoakland.org/wp-content/uploads/2015/07/EDDA_Research-Brief_Digital-Literacy_R.pdf

Middaugh, E. (2016). The social and emotional components of gaming. A response to "the challenge of gaming for democratic education". *Democracy and Education, 24*(2), Article 8. Retrieved March 25, 2017, from democracyeducationjournal.org/home/vol24/iss2/8

Middaugh, E. (2018). Civic media literacy in a transmedia world: Balancing personal experience, factual accuracy and emotional appeal as media consumers and circulators. *Journal of Media Literacy Education, 10*(2), 33–52. Retrieved from https://digitalcommons.uri.edu/jmle/vol10/iss2/3

Middaugh, E., & Evans, C. (2018). Did you know?!...Cultivating online public voice in youth. *Theory and Research in Social Education, 46,* 574–602. https://doi.org/10.1080/00933104.2018.1474059

Middaugh, E., Bowyer, B., & Kahne, J. (2016). U suk! Norms of online political discourse and the implications for adolescent civic development and engagement. *Youth & Society* (Advance online publication). doi:10.1177/0044118X16655246

Rosenberg, R., Baughman, S., & Bailenson, J. (2013). Virtual Superheroes: Using superpowers in virtual reality to encourage prosocial behavior. *PLoS ONE, 8*(1), e55003. doi:10.1371/journal.pone.0055003

Sakr, M., Jewitt, C., & Price, S. (2016). Mobile experiences of historical place: A multimodal analysis of emotional engagement. *Journal of the Learning Sciences, 25*(1), 51–92. http://dx.doi.org/10.1080/10508406.2015.1115761

Smith, S. (2016). Explore everything with Pokemon Go [Blog post]. Autism Pedagogy. Retrieved March 25, 2017, http://www.autismpedagogy.com/blog/2016/7/10/explore-everything-with-pokemon-go

Soep, L. (2014). *Participatory politics: Next generation tactics to remake public spheres* (The John D. & Catherine T. MacArthur Foundation Reports on Digital Media and Learning). Cambridge, MA: MIT Press.

Steinkuhler, C., & Williams, D. (2006). Where everybody knows your (screen) name: Online games as "third places". *Journal of Computer-Mediated Communication, 11*, 885–909.

Stoddard, J., Banks, A. M., Nemacheck, C., & Wenska, E. (2016). The challenges of gaming for democratic education: The Case Of iCivics. *Democracy and Education, 24*(2), Article 2. Retrieved from http://democracyeducationjournal.org/home/vol24/iss2/2

Watt, M., Richardson, P., Klusman, U., Kunter, M., Beyer, B., Trautwein, U., & Baumer, J. (2012). Motivations for choosing teaching as a career: An international comparison using the FIT-Choice scale. *Teaching and Teacher Education, 6*, 791–805. https://doi.org/10.1016/j.tate.2012.03.003

Watts, R. J., Diemer, M. A., & Voight, A. M. (2011). Critical consciousness: Current status and future directions. *New Directions for Child and Adolescent Development, 134*, 43–57. doi:10.1002/cd.310

Youniss, J., & Yates, M. (1997). *Community service and social responsibility.* Chicago, IL: University of Chicago Press.

CHAPTER 6

Projective Worlds: Minecraft and MCAlagaësia

Laura D'Aveta

1 Overarching Questions

1. Which spaces (physical, textual, and imagined) are important to your students? How is that importance expressed?
2. Which spaces are privileged in schools, and how do we make more room for the other spaces?
3. How can mapping in fantasy (and other) texts be leveraged as a text in and of itself in the classroom?

2 Introduction

All reading happens in places. There are the physical locations in which we read: classrooms, coffee shops, a favorite chair by the fire. There are the places of the texts we read: settings, fictional or otherwise, where we journey alongside protagonists and fend off foes; in the genre of fantasy, those places are often shown to us through maps. And there are the places in between: the places in our minds, explored in our imaginations as we read, and often long after.

This chapter will consider an elaborate project in which an adolescent reader and several other fans, who identify themselves as the "MCAlagaësia Team", were in the process of recreating the fantasy world of Alagaësia, the setting of Christopher Paolini's *The Inheritance Cycle*, within the computer game *Minecraft*. The findings suggest that readers are projecting themselves into this digital world and developing a unique sense of place: a projective world (D'Aveta, 2016).

This chapter examines the transmediation of the map of Alagaësia, from text to digital medium, as evidence of a connection between the reader and the setting of the novels and the projection of that reader's sense of place of their own world *into* that setting. In creating a virtual retelling of Paolini's map of Alagaësia, the members of the MCAlagaësia project are creating a virtual reality that not only reflects their own sense of place of the fantasy setting, but also enables other readers and fans of the series to likewise explore the setting of *The Inheritance Cycle* as a unique virtual reality. The interactivity afforded by the *Minecraft* platform creates an opportunity to further examine the projective world created by the MCAlagaësia team as a site for the participatory culture described by Henry Jenkins (1992),[1] resulting in the genesis of additional projective worlds.

The exploration of these projective worlds has the potential to expand our understanding of the ways in which readers engage in fictional worlds, the influence of their own sense of place have in the development of projective worlds, and role of readers as co-creators of these projective worlds.

3 Statement of Problem

Much of the literature surrounding the maps included in fantasy texts relates to the creation of verisimilitude on the part of an implied reader (Iser, 1974), and maps are often evaluated based on whether they are successful in that endeavor. Distinctions are made between maps of primary worlds and secondary worlds; maps that are parallel to the narrative and maps that are a part of the narrative (i.e. the Marauder's Map in *Harry Potter and the Prisoner of Azkaban*); maps that are meant to appear geographical and maps that are metaphorical. The problem with the literature is that the voice of each individual reader is silenced. Missing from these discussions is the map that exists only between an individual reader and the text; the map that the reader sees, which harbors within its lines and latitudes the identity of that reader and his or her sense of place of the actual world and the secondary world; the map whose genesis relies upon the immersion of a reader who carries his or her unique understanding of the world on the journey into that secondary world. The voice of the individual reader is replaced with that of an implied reader – an identity that assumes all readers of fantasy will interact with the text and its paratextual maps in the same manner. The individual reader's participation is dismissed; his or her role as a participant, a co-creator, is ignored.

4 Review of the Relevant Literature

Although not the first author to include a map as part of his work, J. R. R. Tolkien is widely acknowledged as the father of fantasy mapping (Ekman, 2013). These maps are often considered to be part of the "paratext" of the novel—Gerard Genette's term for the extra-narrative material included with a novel, such as the cover, illustrations, and end papers (cited in Magnusson, 2012)—rather than part of the narrative itself; however, the reason for their existence is generally agreed; fantasy maps aid in the creation of verisimilitude (Ekman, 2013; Tolkien, 1964/2001).

In describing the settings of fantasy novels, the terms primary world and secondary world—coined by Tolkien—are those used most often to establish boundaries. Ekman (2013) adds an additional layer of distinction to Tolkien's concept of primary and secondary worlds. For Ekman, there exists the actual world—that is, the world inhabited by the author and the reader; the primary world—the world that is similar to the actual world at the beginning of the story; and the secondary world—the fantasy world. A novel may have multiple secondary worlds, but only one primary world, if any; a novel may exist entirely within a secondary world or worlds. Tolkien's *The Hobbit* and *Lord of the Rings* are set entirely in the secondary world of Middle-earth; *The Wizard of Oz* and *The Lion, the Witch and the Wardrobe* are examples of novels set in a primary world where characters are then transported into the secondary worlds of Oz and Narnia, respectively. Finally, there are novels where the secondary world bleeds into the primary world, rather than (or in addition to) the characters being transported to the secondary world, such as the Harry Potter novels where the magic world intersects the Muggle world while remaining undetected. No work of fantasy is ever set in the actual world; only non-fiction could make such a claim, problematic though such a claim might be.

One of the hallmarks of fantasy literature is its ability to transport the reader into the setting of the novel, not as an observer, but an active participant—a co-creator—of that world. The map is an integral part of that transport, taking advantage of the reader's familiarity with its purpose of understanding a geographical "reality" and therefore adding validity to the reader's experience of the setting of the novel; it is, as Ekman states, meant to aid in "the construction of an internally consistent world" (2013, p. 14). The term verisimilitude is peppered throughout the literature pertaining to fantasy maps, and these maps are often evaluated on their ability to transport a reader into the secondary world. These evaluations, however, are text-centric, focusing on the map itself, rather than the interaction a reader has with the map. The responsibility is placed on the shoulders of the author (and, to some degree, the artist/cartographer), and the reader's role in the interaction is relegated to an implied reader (Iser, 1974) who is a passive observer of the novel's landscape, as though watching it from the window of a commuter train.

Written in 1938–1939—around the time *The Lord of the Rings* was being developed and long before ideas such as reader response theory and participatory culture—and published in 1964, Tolkien's *On Fairy-Stories* is perhaps the most frequently quoted piece of scholarship relating to the uniqueness and importance of fantasy settings. In this landmark essay Tolkien sets forth the idea of the fantasy setting being a secondary world, and also clarifies that the author is in partnership with the reader (in his example, specifically a child reader of fantasy); the author is a "sub-creator" who must provide a secondary world that is so artfully created that the reader believes it, while inside it. Tolkien's writings, both scholarly and fictional,[2] offered the belief that author and reader are co-creators. The secondary world does not exist without the presence of the reader, nor is it constructed without the reader's participation. To speak of the place of a fantasy novel is to speak of both the creator and those who journey through it.

Place may most simply be defined as a space made meaningful. Yi-Fu Tuan, a scholar in the field of humanistic geography, writes that "we are aware of the openness, freedom, and threat of space, and vice versa. Furthermore, if we think of space as that which allows movement, then place is pause; each pause in movement makes it possible for location to be transformed into place" (1977, p. 6). Place is created when an identity has paused to linger within a space, forming an attachment between that identity and that space. The reader's interaction with the primary and secondary worlds of a fantasy novel, his or her immersion in that setting, are a moment of pause, wherein the reader develops a sense of place for that world—what I have termed the projective world.[3]

The theories of place offered by Tuan and humanistic geography describe how an individual might develop a sense of place, but they alone do not address how this occurs when a reader is interacting with a text. Humanistic geography tends to focus on interactions of individuals and spaces in the actual world. Reader response theory renders Tuan's work relevant to secondary worlds.

Influential in both literary theory and literacy, Rosenblatt's *The Reader, the Text, the Poem* (1978) described the transaction between a reader and a text, defining aesthetic reading as the reader being immersed in the text, creating a "poem" – a new text born of the transaction between the reader and text. Differing from literary theories prior to the 1960s and 1970s, the work of Rosenblatt and other reader response theorists emphasized that meaning lay not only within the text itself, but within the transaction between the reader *and* the text; both the text and the reader played a role in the construction of meaning. Scholars have chosen different ways to write about the interaction between reader and text—what Rosenblatt referred to as "poesis" (1978). In writing about videogames as texts, James Gee (2007) describes the three identities involved in the transaction that takes place when an individual is playing a role-playing game, such as *World of Warcraft*: there is the identity of the player; the identity of the avatar – the template character a player modifies when playing the game; and finally, there is the identity of the player-as-character, what Gee refers to as the projective identity. There is a transaction that occurs during game play, not unlike the transaction Rosenblatt describes during aesthetic reading that results in a new identity – the projective identity – that is the unique combination of the game player/reader and the video game character/text. In much the same way, the setting of the text, as it is read aesthetically, is unique to that reader in that particular, contextualized transaction. The reader projects not only his or her identity into the game; I would argue that the reader's sense of place—of the actual world, or of the secondary world if the reader has encountered it in another form, such as a novel or film in the case of Tolkien's *Lord of the Rings*—is also projected into the game. The setting of the text, the secondary world, becomes a projective world.

By considering the reader as having a role in the creation of the secondary world, the scholarship pertaining to fantasy mapping need no longer be limited to consideration of an implied reader. Instead, the individual reader's sense of place—the projective world—is included in the conversations surrounding these secondary worlds. The map that appears at the beginning of a fantasy novel is indelibly changed once readers have projected themselves into the text, in the same manner that Rosenblatt's text is forever changed by the reading transaction. Therein we find the importance of providing space for the individual reader's voice to describe their sense of place of the secondary world—to describe that projective world. What this project demonstrates is that the map now represents a unique projective world for each participant, one that has meaning beyond the moments when they are reading (or rereading as is the case with most of them) the *Inheritance Cycle*. To view the map of Alagaësia as a representation of the secondary world of *The Inheritance Cycle* is now inaccurate as it suggests the meaning is held within the text of the map, rather than the poesis between reader and map; it overlooks, to use Rosenblatt's term, the aesthetic reading of the map; the reader's voice is silenced, the projective world forgotten.

Scholarship pertaining to fantasy maps ends with the secondary world and verisimilitude. Although some scholars will consider the metaphorical or allegorical themes expressed in an author's secondary world, the discussion still ultimately centers on the secondary world and its meaning. Missing is the projective world—specifically, the reader's sense of place of this secondary world that is created when the reader first interacts with the secondary world and continues to grow and evolve thereafter, never fully formed, always becoming, much as the reader's identity is never complete. At best, scholarship may consider the identity of an implied reader; such scholars focus on a generalized "fantasy reader" who is assumed to interact with the text in a prescribed manner. The reader's participation in the co-creation—or perhaps, co-discovery—of the novel's setting is notably absent.

5 Narrative of Context and Approach

The goal of my research was to understand how maps in fantasy novels might be considered to have purpose beyond creating verisimilitude—to extend the existing scholarship in a way that would observe, describe and interpret the ways in which readers of a fantasy series interacted with that series' fantasy map. Such interactions were examined as potential evidence of the reader having developed a sense of place for the secondary world of Alagaësia—as evidence of a projective world. This understanding would create a space within the literature relating to fantasy maps that acknowledged the reader's voice and the possibility that fantasy maps represent more than secondary worlds for implied readers.

I was aware, as a scholar of young adult literature, that Christopher Paolini was an adolescent at the time *Eragon,* the first novel in *The Inheritance Cycle,* was written. With the theoretical framework of projective worlds growing from my emphasis on the importance of the child's voice, my interest in the concept of a fantasy map representing a child's/adolescent's sense of place being critical in the development of a secondary world naturally led to a desire to work with participants who, as children, had created fantasy maps. Paolini presented an opportunity to interview an author who fit those parameters. During his interview, Paolini provided images that represented the evolution of the map of Alagaësia, including the first draft, shown below (see Figure 6.1).

During my interviews of Paolini, he mentioned the subject of fan art, and I learned of the existence of "retellings" of the map of Alagaësia made by fans. This represented another source of data, and the scope of the research project was expanded to include fans. With Paolini's cooperation, digital communications were sent out to his fan base via Twitter and Facebook, requesting that interested parties visit a website I had created in order to learn a bit about the project and indicate their interest in participating. If they submitted their name and email address, they were selected for interviews. There were two phases to the interviews conducted with fans of *The Inheritance Cycle*. The first was designed to identify characteristics, if any, in the participants that met those of the scholarly implied reader of fantasy, and to begin asking questions about how the participants interacted with the map of Alagaësia. The second interviews were conducted with those participants who demonstrated an engagement with the map of Alagaësia that occurred at times other than

FIGURE 6.1   Paolini's first map of Alagaësia

when they were reading the books. All interviews were conducted via e-mail to accommodate the fans' locations around the world. It was through these methods that I encountered one of the founders of the MCAlagaësia team.

At sixteen, Firnen represented one of the youngest participants in the project. A tenth grader in Canberra, Australia, he described reading habits and preferences that an implied reader of fantasy would. Firnen stated that one of the most important aspects of fantasy is that it must "transport you to another time or place where your imagination can run free" (Firnen, *Interview Part One*). He further spoke of the same verisimilitude that the scholarship mentions: "[T]o create a good fantasy book, the author should put a lot of effort into world building. Not a 'boring' or 'uninteresting' world like our own, but one that readers *want* to believe in" (ibid.). Firnen further described the ability of fantasy to transport the reader into the narrative—to allow for the creation of a projective world:

For me, the best part about reading fantasy is to be transported to another world. A good author who has spent a lot of time and effort building their world can make a reader not only believe in the world that they are trying to create, but imagine themselves in that world too, with the characters and exploring the places. (Firnen, *Interview Part One*)

One of the questions in the first interview asked participants whether or not they had created any artwork "inspired by or related to the map of Alagaësia" (*Interview Packet Part One*). Firnen's response dismisses his interactions with the map of Alagaësia, briefly mentioning spending "about 30 hours staring at the map of Alagaësia whilst painting the terrain for MCAlagaësia in World-Painter" (Firnen, *Interview Part* One).

The "MC" of "MCAlagaësia" that Firnen refers to is the computer game *Minecraft*, a survival-themed game where players interact with their environment by cultivating dwellings, weapons, and other tools out of "blocks" of materials available in the game, and represents the majority of Firnen's interactions with Paolini's original map of Alagaësia. A screencap of MCAlagaësia's work is shown in Figure 6.2; note the similarities between their map and Paolini's map of Alagaësia (Figure 6.1). At the time of our interviews, the creation of MCAlagaësia was still in its infancy, and was not open to having players interact with the secondary world beyond construction tasks. Firnen described the genesis of MCAlagaësia and its development through several iterations/versions.

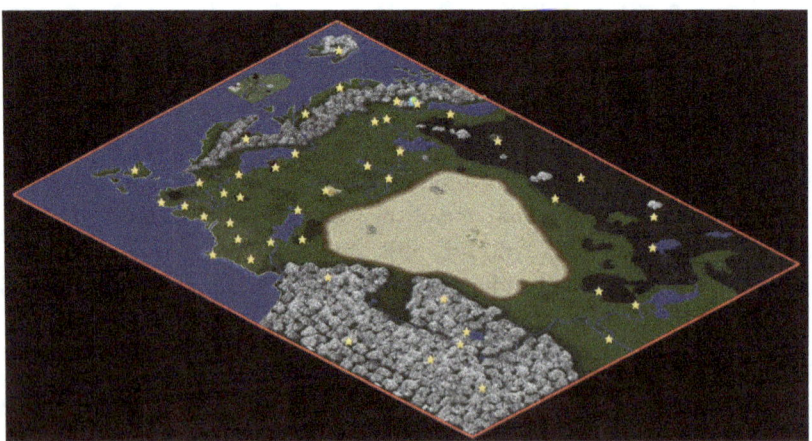

FIGURE 6.2 The MCAlagaësia team's map of Alagaësia in Minecraft

Firnen's reasons for recreating Alagaësia in *Minecraft* suggest that when he views the map of Alagaësia, he is now seeing a projective world. "…[W]e thought Alagaësia was a rich and vivid world, and we knew we could create something unique with it. We had seen other projects that attempt to recreate lands [from other works of fantasy]. Nobody had attempted to create Alagaësia, so this was a new challenge" (Firnen, *Interview Part Two*). The amount of time Firnen has invested in the project and his descriptions of the work performed illustrate his role as co-creator in the secondary world of Alagaësia:

> I've spent hours in *WorldPainter* tracing over the map multiple times, raising mountains and carving rivers. Through this, I've learned more about the geography of this land than I could have simply reading these books. Overall, this project and interacting with the map makes me think more deeply about the entire series and Alagaësia. (Firnen, *Interview Part Two*)

Firnen and the rest of the MCAlagaësia team, which now numbers in the thirties, have devoted dozens, if not hundreds, of hours to the recreation of the map of Alagaësia in *Minecraft*. Due to the immersive quality of the *Minecraft* game, what appears as a simple, pixilated map (Figure 6.2) is actually a detailed, interactive environment built from nothing, requiring the reimagining of a two-dimensional drawing in a three-dimensional landscape. The devotion to accuracy described by Firnen and present in the website devoted to the recreation of Alagaësia in *Minecraft*,[4] signifies a deep connection to the secondary world of *The Inheritance Cycle* that clearly casts the MCAlagaësia team in the role of co-creators.

In recreating the setting of *The Inheritance Cycle* in a 3-D digital environment, Firnen and his team are expressing their projective world. Their work continues to expand inward; with the overall framework of the map having been established, the MCAlagaësia team now works to "zoom in" on each area to build intricate micro-settings, as detailed as the furniture in Eragon's chambers or the specific dimensions of the mountain fortress of Farthen Dûr. Firnen is focused on the ability of MCAlagaësia to create a sense of immersion, for themselves and for all those who would journey into MCAlagaësia.

In true participatory culture form, Firnen and the MCAlagaësia team are co-creators, sharing their projective world with other fans using *Minecraft* as their platform. Their engagement with text extends the boundaries of literacy beyond those drawn by pedagogy to include videogames and graphic design, and by extension programming and other STEM-related subjects. The amount of work required to build a world in *Minecraft* is onerous, and the team's decision to recruit other fans to assist in its design and construction reflects the cooperative nature of fan bases described by Jenkins (1992). The immersion of readers in fantasy worlds presents the potential to integrate reading into subjects beyond the language arts in ways that are engaging and meaningful to students and teachers alike.

6   Conclusion

All of the participants in this study—whether author or reader, artist or critic, or, more often, bricolages of several identities—have acknowledged this consensus belief in the map's ability to create verisimilitude on behalf of the reader. They describe referring back to the map of Alagaësia to track the movement of characters throughout the narrative; they are familiar with other fantasy works that also contain maps; and they often have experience, as writers of texts, with the role a map can play in the genesis of a world. Their familiarity with the genre was expected, as they were recruited through their identity as fans of a fantasy series; the participants in my study could easily be cast in the role of the implied reader that the literature surrounding the genre of fantasy presents. Yet these participants had described experiences that went beyond what the implied reader is described as having experienced. The secondary world of Alagaësia was unique for each of them, and as individuals, it was incorrect to assume that their uniformity of understanding of the purpose of a fantasy map equated to a uniformity of *perception* of the fantasy map. After all, if a map is a text, and each reader's interaction with that text creates a new text (poesis, in Rosenblatt's, 1978, terminology), then the artifact they saw when looking at the map of Alagaësia could no longer be representative of a secondary world alone. Rather, the map of Alagaësia, as read by a participant, is a palimpsest; a multilayered artifact that represents a reader's experience of immersing themselves in the secondary world, bringing with them their experiences of the actual world; it is now a map of a projective world—projective, rather than "projected", because each interaction with the map, each immersion in the secondary world, each new experience in the actual world, and in the case of a participatory cultural context, each interaction with other readers, players, or fans; all of these add new layers to the palimpsest.

A secondary world does not exist without a reader. Although Paolini may have created the map of Alagaësia, he is not wholly responsible for its existence. The deep roots of the fantasy genre, of which Paolini was a fan, fed his work in creating the map of Alagaësia; and after what may be perceived as the end of his role as creator of the secondary world—its publication and "release" to readers—Alagaësia continued to grow, a palimpsest upon which each reader would add their own layer.

To think of Alagaësia as a secondary world is to exclude the role the readers have in its existence; to place the text in a position of authority; to deny the collaboration between author and reader in the formation of the text. Instead, each reader must be considered a co-creator of Alagaësia; for each participant, and for all who interact with the map and accompanying narrative, Alagaësia is a projective world.

Notes

1. Tolkien's story *Leaf by Niggle* has at its heart the theme of co-creation.
2. The participants' names, with the exception of the author's name, were changed to protect their identities. The participants chose their pseudonyms from the characters in *The Inheritance Cycle*.
3. The term *projective* used in this section is not derived from the cartographical term "projection", which relates to the representation of any celestial sphere onto a plane surface. Rather, it relates to the writings of James Gee and is more fully defined in the latter portion of this section.
4. See www.MCAlagaësia.com

References

D'Aveta, L. (2016). *In search of Alagaësia: Exploring the conjunction of reader, author and place in Christopher Paolini's the inheritance cycle* (Unpublished doctoral dissertation). Pennsylvania State University, State College, PA.

Ekman, S. (2013). *Here be dragons: Exploring fantasy maps and settings*. Middletown, CT: Wesleyan University Press.

Gee, J. (2007). *What video games have to teach us about learning and literacy*. New York, NY: Palgrave Macmillan.

Iser, W. (1974). *The implied reader: Patterns of communication in prose fiction from Bunyan to Beckett*. Baltimore, MD: The Johns Hopkins University Press.

Jenkins, H. (1992). *Textual poachers: Television fans & participatory culture*. New York, NY: Routledge.

Magnusson, K. (2012). Lemony Snickett's a series of unfortunate events: Daniel Handler and marketing the author. *Children's Literature Association Quarterly, 37*(1), 86–107.

Rosenblatt, L. (1978). *The reader, the text, the poem: The transactional theory of the literary work*. Carbondale, IL: Southern Illinois University Press.

Tolkien, J. R. R. (2001). *Tree and leaf*. London: HarperCollins Publishers. (Original work published 1964)

Tuan, Y. (1977). *Space and place: The perspective of experience*. Minneapolis, MN: University of Minnesota Press.

CHAPTER 7

Literacy Practice and Play: Participatory Culture in the MMORPG, *FFXIV: A Realm Reborn*

Shannon R. Mortimore-Smith

1   Overarching Questions

1. How can educators foster classroom environments that value participatory culture in the same way that online games do?
2. In what way can our classroom curriculum be tailored to encourage and to facilitate new literacy competencies?
3. What can the participatory culture of online games teach adolescents about their own agency, identity, creativity, and problem-solving skills in both the real and virtual worlds?
4. How might we leverage the shared narratives and social connections developed in online role-playing games in the physical space of our classrooms?
5. How can our students become "insiders, teachers, and producers" (Gee, 2007, p. 212) of the content they study?

2   Introduction

Without a doubt, videogames—from *Pong* to *Pokemon* to *Portal*—from *Final Fantasy* to First-Person-Shooters to *Four Square*—have captivated millions of players. According to one report from the Pew Research Center, 81% of teens ages 13 to 17 own or have access to game consoles like the Xbox 360, the PS4, and the Wii (Lenhart, 2015). A second study concludes that, "almost all teens play games" (para 2). Seventy-six percent of these teens indicated that videogames are a means to connect socially with others, either by gaming with peers in the same room or by engaging with other gamers in online spaces (Lenhart et al., 2008). Game designer McGonigal reports in her TED talk, "Gaming Can Make a Better World" (2010) that by the age of 21, the average gamer has logged 10,000 hours of play time—roughly equivalent to the number of hours a child spends in school from fifth grade through high school graduation. Massively Multiplayer Online Role Playing Games (MMORPGs) like *World of Warcraft* and

Final Fantasy XIV: A Realm Reborn, report millions of paid subscribers each year, and the popularity of these games only continues to rise. As McGonigal (2010) suggests, videogames have become a kind of "parallel education" in the United States. Of those who play online role-playing games, nearly 25% are reported to be between the ages of 12 and 19 (Yee, 2009). For this reason alone, it is imperative that educators study the value of videogames in young people's lives and evaluate their potential for inspiring engaged and meaningful literacy practices both within the virtual world and without.

Videogames themselves, specifically role-playing games (RPGs), allow adolescents to explore their identity, to investigate alternative worlds, to create and to collaborate with others, to communicate textually and through the performance of their selected avatar, and to participate in out-of-game community and fan-based forums. Videogames, like good classrooms, are highly structured environments with clearly defined goals. Players meet these goals by learning to communicate and collaborate with others to achieve desirable outcomes. Most often, success requires a commitment to experimentation, a willingness to openly embrace failure, and a deep knowledge of the diverse strengths and weaknesses that each member of the guild, or team, brings to each new encounter.

Further, immersion in these games—and the literacy practices that emerge as a result of this immersion—is enhanced through highly sensorial and multimodal environments. The visual imagery, the music and sound effects, the spatial placement of the avatar within the world, and his/her ability to interact with and manipulate the game environment, creates a feeling of "being there"—of no longer "playing a game" but of being inside of it. Players embody these worlds; they are agents capable of enacting meaningful outcomes, and they are empowered through their ability to do so. American literary theorist and philosopher Burke argued that young people should read books because it provides them with "imaginative rehearsals" for the real world—rehearsals that allow them to engage in the complex world of ideas and "wrestle with the issues that remain universal in our lives" (as cited in Gallagher, 2009, p. 66). Videogames can do the same—perhaps, arguably, in more compelling ways. Rather than contemplating outcomes, gamers enact them.

Aside from what we intuitively know about games, games are fun, they engage us in ways that bring us intrinsic pleasure and joy, they foster a sense of community, collaboration, and healthy competition, and they provide us with a well-deserved release from the tedium and responsibilities of our daily lives, video games—particularly good video games—can do so much more. In his TED talk, Gabe Zichermann (2011), author of *Game-Based Marketing*, argues that engaging in videos games increases "Fluid Intelligence". According to Zichermann, gamers "seek novelty"—they want games to show them something new, unique, and exciting. They "think creatively and challenge themselves"—games present players with a variety of stimulating obstacles and they give players the tools and feedback necessary to successfully tackle these obstacles. Gamers, "do things the hard way"—they seek more and increasingly difficult challenges that will put their skill to the test, and finally, they provide a way for players to "network" by sharing experiences and solving problems together, collaboratively (Zichermann, 2011). As both scholars and gamers testify, work in videogames is rewarding. It is work that gives a sense of immediate purpose, achievement, and personal satisfaction. Unfortunately, it is also the kind of work that is too often missing from our classrooms, from our jobs, and from our participation in the "real" world. As educators we must to be prepared to move with our students into the 21st-century by recognizing that in literacy "shift happens" (Zichermann, 2011). MMORPGs, like *Final Fantasy XIV: A Realm Reborn,* allow young people to engage in a series of "imaginative rehearsals" that allow them to sharpen their values and think meaningfully about the impact of their choices. Given the digital age that we live in and the 21st-century learners that we serve as educators, we must begin to rethink current classroom practice and seriously consider the value of online role-playing games as valid literacy landscapes.

3   Welcome to Eorzea

Game company Square Enix, under the direction of producer, Naoki Yoshida, launched *A Realm Reborn* in August 2013. With servers located in the United States, Europe, and Japan, the game currently boasts nearly five million subscribers worldwide, and enjoys a devoted, multicultural and multigenerational player base. The game is currently available for play on PC Microsoft Windows, Mac OS X, and PlayStation 4. Upon its release, game reviewers from PC Gamer, Kotaku, and IGN praised the game's "epic, twisting storylines and magical landscapes", "gorgeously rendered and beautifully orchestrated" fantasy lands, and "excitingly varied and flexible class system". Players who enter the world of Eorzea, begin by selecting one of three city-states to begin their adventure: Gridania, a vast, thickly-wooded forest, rich in greenery, rife with magic, and led by the Elder Seedseer, Kan-E-Sanna; Ul'dah, a wealthy merchant-oasis surrounded by hot desert sands and led by the Sultana, Nanamo Ul'Namo and the Syndicate Elite General, Raubaun; or Limsa Lominsa, a pirate-marine state, settled on the ancient cliffs of the Rhotano Sea and ruled by Admiral Merlwyb Bloefhiswyn.

Players of MMORPGS are additionally required to create a character—an avatar or second skin—to maneuver through the game world. With a wealth of options, players typically begin by choosing the gender and race of their characters, then decide which "class" or role the character will play within the realm. In the world of Eorzea in *Final Fantasy XIV,* players initially have the option to choose from five different races: the Hyur, a human race; Elezen, tall, slender elves; the Rogadyn, a robust, warrior-like race; the Miqo'te, a playful, feline race, and the Lalafell, a diminutive race with child-like features. In addition to selecting their race, players have the ability to sculpt the physical appearance of their avatars—and here no detail is too minute. Everything from skin color to eye color, to the shape of the nose, brow, and jawline are thoroughly attended to. Scars, tattoos, and birthmarks, character height and girth, breast size, hair color, and makeup are all carefully selected to adorn the "second self". Many players choose to create characters with features similar to their own. Yet the avatar is typically a "best self"—one who gamers might like to imagine they can be, rather than who they truly are.

Once players have selected their chosen city and identity, they are additionally asked to select a suitable job or class to play within the game. Following tradition, *Final Fantasy XIV* [*FFXIV*] includes class roles that are prominently featured in all of the Final Fantasy titles published by the franchise. These classes, with names like White Mage, Black Mage, Paladin, Monk, Dragoon, Warrior, and Summoner, each fulfill a specific function within the game. Paladins and Warriors, for example, serve as protectors in the game, preventing other players from taking damage from enemies. The White Mage heals party members, and Monks, Dragoons, and Black Mages damage or kill attacking enemies. In this sense, *FFXIV* participates in what many MMORPGS recognize as the Trinity or Triad, a balanced combination of class roles and abilities comprised by tanks, healers, and damage-dealers. Each role is crucial for the success of the entire group within the party. Groups attempting to perform with any role absent from the triad generally face defeat. In this way, collaboration with fellow players and a basic understanding of how each role contributes to the success of the triad, is necessary for the advancement of the individual player overall. Unlike single-player role-playing games, progression in MMORPGS is highly incumbent upon the ability of individual players to band together in skilled groups in order to achieve desirable outcomes. To accomplish this level of success, players join Free Companies (FCs) or guilds, designed to unite single-players into powerful multiplayer groups, capable of taking on the increasingly difficult challenges presented by the game itself.

Once a player has a body or a "second skin" and a specific role to maneuver through the game, immersion in the game world becomes second nature. In groups as small as 4, known as a "light party" and as large as 24, more typically called a "raid", players team together to tackle "dungeons" where they fight groups of "mobs" or roaming monsters. These monsters drop "loot" that benefit the players and they also give "XP" or experience points. Each dungeon contains three or more "bosses", whose defeat requires players to be knowledgeable both with one another's skills and with a variety of difficult game mechanics. Players typically earn better gear or rare items as a reward for completing these dungeons, along with the ability to progress into new dungeons and complete even harder content.

Yet beyond the reward inherent within these set mechanics, players in MMORPGs reap social rewards as well. When a difficult goal is achieved, individual players share the opportunity to celebrate their accomplishments alongside their guildmates and online friends. A sense of community is established between players in their efforts to achieve such goals together. Oftentimes, teams work not only for the benefit of the individual or for the progression of the game's storyline, but for the growth and improvement of the unit overall. This kind of gameplay requires establishing meaningful goals, communicating them clearly to the entire unit, coordinating player skills effectively, and attending to the social morale of the group as a whole. Collectively, the unit is much more powerful than the individual in an MMORPG. Further, friendly social interaction, shared praise, and good-natured hazing between guildmates makes this space a place where players want to come back, not only to experience the game itself, but to enjoy the game and its challenges alongside the company and companionship of peers.

4   Research Methodology

As a player and a guild member in *FFXIV* for nearly seven years, and as a literacy educator for twenty years, my research goal for this study was to better understand the gameplay experiences of the adolescent members within the *FFXIV* community. Through Participant Observation (Spradley, 1980) it was my hope to learn more about these players by playing alongside them. My own personal experiences and observations as an avid player within the game might thereby allow me to unearth the relevance of *FFXIV* for sponsoring playful literacy practices and fostering participatory culture. As an autoethnographer immersed in the culture of *FFXIV*, I actively confronted this research as an engaged participant. According to Ellis and Bochner (2000), research conducted in this way allows, "the research text [to become] the story, complete (but open) in itself, and largely free of academic jargon and theory" (p. 745).

For this study, I interviewed "Soleil", a high school student, who has been playing the game since 2014. Her stories comprise the primary framework for this research. To augment her experiences, I additionally invited teenaged gamers outside of my guild to share their gameplay experiences in the r/ffxiv Reddit forum, established to support the interests of the online FFXIV gaming community as a whole.

5   Gaming with Soleil

"It was my brother and his more masculine hobbies and pursuits that first persuaded me to play FFXIV", said my guildmate, "Soleil", a seventeen-year-old high school senior. She began playing the game in 2014, at the age of fourteen, though she admitted that she has been playing free online MMORPGs since the age of ten. When I asked her what interested her in the game she said, "I stick around for the community, and for the story. I like playing games where you're the good, omniscient hero". Outside of the game Soleil, an all-A's student, indicated that she loves fantasy stories. She reads fan fictions and even aspires to write her own fantasy novels, and she uses the game world and environments in FFXIV to help inspire her. "In real life I have limited travel experience", said Soleil, "but I love exploring the scenery in FFXIV. It helps me to design the worlds that I write about in my own stories". Soleil also enjoys drawing, and she uses the character creation screen in the game to help improve her own technique. Soleil, who "likes to think that [she] works hard", plays the violin and plans to study medicine in college. When I asked her more about her goals, she shared that her career interests were "partially inspired by her time in game, meeting people who had needs in the community, and wanting to help them". While her experiences in game have been largely positive, she does confess, that sometimes she feels like she's "wasted time" playing games and that "games are not seen as beneficial to society as a whole".

"Soleil", a Highlander Hyur, is the name of my guildmate's third avatar. When I met Soleil, two years ago, she was a female Lalafell by another name, and she later changed again to a male Au'Ra (dragonborn) named "Drelin". Regarding these three online identities, Soleil said she uses her avatars as a way to develop the characters in her own stories. She also shared that her avatars were a way of helping her to experiment with the developmental phases in her own life. "As a male avatar, I wanted to be tall and intimidating. Drelin had horns, and Drelin was the name of the first MMORPG avatar I played. I tried to recreate him". When she "got bored with Drelin, because he was a dude", Soleil began exploring her identity as a female avatar, and she admits that shifting between these fluid gender identities allowed her to experiment with her own identity in safe, casual ways. Because "there were no consequences for [experimenting] in a video game", Soleil shared that her avatars were a way of "slowly working out" and experimenting with her own sexual orientation as well.

In her gameplay today, Soleil says that it is both the challenge that the game provides and her community of friends within the guild that persuade her to log-in. While she is the youngest member of our guild, (most of us are in our late-twenties or thirties), she says, "I prefer playing with the old folks. The environment is much more relaxed, and people forgive me easier for mistakes that I make". Overall, Soleil shares that *FFXIV* allows her to "release her creativity and broaden her imagination", and as her guildmate of four years, I can validate that her presence in the guild makes us stronger as a whole.

6   Online Role-Playing Games as Participatory Culture

Online role-playing games are additionally unique in the sense that the more a player participates in the online realm, the more opportunities for shared narratives and experiences and social connections emerge. In *Final Fantasy XIV: A Realm Reborn*, each player's avatar is referred to within the game as the "Warrior of Light". The warrior's role within the realm is to contribute her "sword" to the greater cause by heroically confronting and quelling the threat of the warring factions that serve as the principal conflict. Through this identity, player-avatars experience flashbacks, called "Echos", that give them insight into the events of the past, and they act at the behest of the non-playing characters or NPCs, whose role is to require the warrior's aid through a variety of in-game quests and missions. This is the *primary* narrative that exists within the game, the story that the game itself is *designed* to tell, and one that each playing character must participate in and "read" in order to progress through the game.

Yet, a more compelling narrative begins to surface the more a player participates in the game: a social narrative that operates solely outside of the constructed "storyline", a narrative built through the collaboration and shared experiences of the people who play the game. In this sense, players—both agents and actors—experience the game in two distinct ways: First, through the story that they *play* and second, through the story that they *construct* with their peers through their mutual, social interactions.

When Soleil logs-in to the game, she greets us through the online text-chat interface, "Hey guys!" She teases her fellow guildmate: "Pyste-Senpai [guild leader], when are we going to try beating Byakko [a "boss"] again? What an epic FAIL that was. Maybe you'll remember to use Shield Oath on your Paladin this time, so you won't get CRUSHED on the first hit, lol". Her reminder of our embarrassing failure causes others to chime in as well. Pyste responds: "I don't know...maybe when you all get gud enough, you scrubs". He jokingly calls himself the "Angry Guild Leader;" he likes to shout commands on Discord, our guild voice chat, while we raid. Sometimes we listen to him, but mostly we die. The more we chat, the more we become swept into the vivid memory of our miserable loss. "I promise I won't die so much this time", I type into the chat. "It's not easy healing when my face is in the floor". My guildmates laugh and attempt to comfort me, demonstrating this in short-cut emoticons typed in the chat bar. "But it's such a pretty face", Soleil chides. I pretend to be miffed, but Soleil has a way of lifting our spirits with her energy and optimism. We make plans to try again on the weekend, and in doing so, we know new stories will emerge. Our memories become our secondary narrative, a more compelling narrative, and ultimately the reason why we enjoy the game and continue to log on each day.

Our fluidity with these identities—to be both the "Warrior of Light" and "that healer with her face planted in the floor"—and our ability to use these identities to shift between these dual game narratives represents one of the many skills identified by Jenkins, Clinton, Purushotma, Robison, & Weisel (2009) as New Media Literacies. According to Jenkins et al. (2009), "Participatory culture shifts the focus of literacy from individual expression to community involvement" (p. 4). Within this framework, the definition of literacy is broadened to include these new competencies:

- *Play*: The capacity to experiment with the surroundings as a form of problem solving.
- *Performance*: The ability to adopt alternative identities for the purpose of improvisation and discovery.
- *Collective intelligence*: The ability to pool knowledge and compare notes with others toward a common goal.
- *Transmedia navigation*: The ability to follow the flow of stories and information across multiple modalities.
- *Negotiation*: The ability to travel across diverse communities, discerning and respecting multiple perspectives, and grasping and following alternative norms (Jenkins, et al., 2009, p. 4).

In our "performance" as both our avatars and ourselves in *FFXIV*, my guildmates and I slip seamlessly between our character lives and our real lives. As a team, we assess each new challenge by weighing our "collective intelligence" and reviewing past experiences. We work together to accomplish difficult tasks that could never be successfully tackled alone, and as we "navigate" the game world, we learn to mediate multiple sources of highly sensorial input. The immersive environments constructed by the game allow us to feel transported, plunged into a new world with sparkling beaches, snow-capped mountains, and ancient forests. The game itself is a multimodal marvel. Soaring across the pink-hued horizon in Dravania on an eagle mount, the music shifts at sunset, signaling the end of another day in Eorzea. Each new area is imbued with its own color palette, its own melody, its own cast. Yet the dimensionality of the game does not end here. 21st-century gamers must also be adept multitaskers, able to interact with the game environment through a complicated user interface and a series of game inventories and menus. Players must learn to communicate with one another through layered, online chat boxes and voice chat systems, and manipulate the game controls in ways that skillfully direct the movements of their avatars inside of the game world, and all of this is happening—all at once. As we "play" we negotiate new territories, new skills, and new relationships in ways that benefit us both within the game world and without.

Similar to the experiences described by my guildmate Soleil, adolescent testimonies posted in the subreddit, r/FFXIV mirror these assertions. In a post titled, "FFXIV gamers ages 13–20, what is your experience with FFXIV and the FFXIV gaming community", teen Redditor "panicalot" writes:

> I'm 13, I've been playing this since I was 11. I've generally had a good experience with the community except for a few times…People have always had trouble adjusting to my voice during raids but that's okay…In FC's I've always been the youngest so I kinda feel like a baby, some people acted like a parent towards me and some treated me normally. I'm an i227 WHM [high-level White Mage] clearing up Savage [currently the most difficult game content]…so I'd say I'm doing pretty well for a 13 year old…What really keeps me playing is the upcoming content, current content, and my friends and FC :)

Another teen Redditor, "RavenShadowmoon" adds:

> I've been playing [*FFXIV*] like it's a second life, it's not a game, I've built a family or two in the game, and I'd help them like they were [family], this game made me find my best friends, but I've also met some rather rude people, like my old fc leader…Overall I've enjoyed it greatly, it's been something to help me get through everyday life.

Similarly, in a post titled, "FFXIV gamers who began gaming or who are currently gaming in your teens", Redditor "JustAlways" shared:

> *FFXIV* was my first rpg I ever played…I was blown away by the community. The biggest surprise was that I am a lot younger than your average

mmorpg player…The interaction with players inside the game is one of the reasons why I play. At first my goals were always to get the best gear and beat all raids, but after some time I started to enjoy leveling and meeting new people.

Like Soleil, these teens acknowledge that while the challenge of the game is a compelling reason for playing the game—and, notably, all of these teens are participating in the most difficult content that the game has to offer—it is the community of players and the relationships that they forge within the game that keep them coming back. By engaging in these forms of participatory culture, "young people are acquiring skills that will serve them well in the future… [skills that rework] the rules by which school, cultural expression, civic life, and work operate" (Jenkins et al., 2009, p. 9). This is further acknowledged by Gee and Hayes (2012), who write, "learning potentially stems from both the game play…and the social practices going on in and around the game, as well as from the interaction between the two" (p. 2). As demonstrated by each of these teens in their own testimonies, and by own gameplay, one key value of participatory culture in MMORPGS is the opportunity for adolescents to rehearse the cultural competencies necessary for successfully navigating the changing landscape of the 21st-century.

7 *FFXIV* Fan Culture as Participatory Culture

Perhaps the greatest example of MMORPGS as participatory culture is evidenced in the fan communities that proliferate outside of the context of the game world itself. In this "metagame" or the "game outside of the game" (Gee & Hayes, 2012, pp. 3–4), players interact socially through their interplay in a wide variety of fan-based, and most often, fan-created "affinity spaces" (Gee & Hayes, 2012). Here their united interests in the game supersede "differences in age, class, race, gender, and educational level", and participants are "motivated to acquire new knowledge or refine their existing skills" through "peer to peer teaching" (Gee, cited in Jenkins et al., 2009, p. 9). Jenkins et al. further note that in a participatory culture, mentorship is valued. As such, gamers "believe that their contributions matter" and "feel a degree of social connection with one another" (Jenkins et al., 2009, p. 8). While MMORPG gamers are often criticized as isolationists, incapable of social interaction in the real world, the copious contributions of the *FFXIV* fan base in online communities prove otherwise. To be a member of the *FFXIV* community not only demonstrates an affinity for the game world itself, but it marks a kinship between the players who enthusiastically participate in the fan culture surrounding the game. These communities provide "low barriers to artistic expression" and uphold "strong support for creating and sharing creations with others" (Jenkins et al., 2009, p. 7).

Players who attend Square Enix sponsored fan festivals, for example, meet and mingle with their online friends and guildmates, many of whom they may have never met "in real life". They participate in live quests and missions, they attend panels with game developers, composers, and story writers. They construct elaborate costumes and engage in cosplay (costume-play) contests, and they submit original artwork in fanart competitions. Beyond these organized events, thousands of other fans contribute their fanart, fanfictions, and cosplays in popular online platforms, hoping to share their love of the game with other enthusiasts and form supportive communities around their mutual interests. DeviantArt, the "largest online social network for artists and art enthusiasts", provides a platform for millions of registered members to "exhibit, promote, and share their works" with others (DeviantArt, n.d.). Contributors, known as "deviants" upload nearly 160,000 original works of art every day (About DeviantArt). A simple search for "FFXIV" in the DeviantArt database yields nearly 19,000 entries of original fanart. Artists who post their work on this site, enjoy the opportunity to network with one another. Talented artists commission their work to fans, while novice contributors simply enjoy sharing their art and receiving positive feedback on their work. Submissions posted by these artists range from paintings, sketches, comics, and digital art. Artists often receive or solicit comments and feedback in their personal user forum, and in this way, the forum itself becomes a community of support. Similarly, other sites like the Lodestone, Fanfiction.net, Tumblr, and Reddit, provide opportunities for fans to share original fiction and creative writing, screenshots, photography, comic strips, craft projects, cooking projects, and theorycrafting related to the game through game blogs, fanfictions, and forum posts. Together, these contributions demonstrate the tremendous outpouring of literacy practices that arise as a result of the enthusiasm these players share for the game, the game world, and for one another. It is, in every way, a community that values the social connection, the sharing and contribution, and the artistic expression that a participatory culture values. Both in the game, and outside of it, players of all ages are asked to be meaning-makers and contributors for the growth of the community at large.

8   Conclusion

To conclude, I would like to invite all educators, whether "hardcore", "casual", or "newbie", to be open to the new literacy possibilities that playing videogames provide for adolescents. While I have yet to find a way for all of my students to play *FFXIV*—and although I admit this is not my greater goal—I do believe that prioritizing playful learning methodologies and fostering a participatory culture within our own classrooms is crucial for achieving meaningful progress.

Like gamers, our students should be given specific, achievable goals. They should encounter pedagogies that teach them that their choices matter, and that there is more than one way to succeed. They should be asked, like gamers in a participatory culture, to create, to think critically, and to collaborate with others to achieve satisfying and personally rewarding outcomes. And when they fail, the consequences for their failure should be minimized so that true discovery, experimentation, and innovation can take wing. Our students, like online gamers, should feel bonded by their shared experiences and endeavors to learn new and challenging content. Their role in our classroom should not be one of mere consumers, but of "insiders, teachers, and producers" (Gee, 2007, p. 212). Most importantly, through their own agency as participants in *classroom* culture, and through the affinity spaces that we create for them as their teachers, our students should understand that their contributions matter.

As teachers too, we must begin the work of constructing a new narrative about the shape of literacy education in the 21st-century. We must resist models of education that have falsely trained our students to believe that educators are the benefactors of all knowledge and that they can never own it for themselves. We must provide "multiple routes" for success (Gee, 2007, p. 105) and offer compelling curricular choices for our students and then teach them how to use these choices to direct their own learning. We must value, and truly listen to, our students' voices and perspectives, and insist that they take ownership for their own ideas. We must be mentors and collaborators and teach our students how to mentor others as well. We must be willing to set the stage for good learning—in the same way that good games do—by providing all of the tools our students need to learn and thrive, and then, we must demand they prove their worth, by letting go. Finally, we must look beyond the borders of traditional literacy practice and invite innovation into our classrooms. Let us too become attuned to the power of play in our lives as educators and log-in to the potential that this new media ignites.

References

DeviantArt. (n.d.). *About Deviantart: Bleed and breed art*. Retrieved from https://about.deviantart.com/

Ellis, C. S., & Bochner, A. (2000). Autoethnography, personal narrative, reflexivity: Research as subject. In N. Denzin & Y. Lincoln (Eds.), *Handbook of qualitative research* (pp. 733–768). Thousand Oaks, CA: Sage.

Gee, J. P. (2007). *What video games have to teach us about learning and literacy.* New York, NY: Palgrave Macmillan.

Gee, J. P., & Hayes, E. (2012). Nurturing affinity spaces and game-based learning. In *Games, learning, and society: Learning and meaning in the digital age.* Retrieved from http://jamespaulgee.com/geeimg/pdfs/Affinity%20Spaces.pdf

Gallagher, K. (2009). *Readicide: How schools are killing reading and what you can do about it.* New York, NY: Stenhouse Publishers.

Jenkins, H., Clinton, K., Purushotma, R., Robison, A. J., & Weigel, M. (2009). *Confronting the challenges of participatory culture: media education for the 21st-century.* Retrieved from https://www.macfound.org/media/article_pdfs/JENKINS_WHITE_PAPER.PDF

Lenhart, A. (2015). *A majority of American teens report access to a computer, game console, smartphone, and a tablet.* Pew Research Center: Internet & Technology. Retrieved from http://www.pewinternet.org/2015/04/09/a-majority-of-american-teens-report-access-to-a-computer-game-console-smartphone-and-a-tablet/

Lenhart, A., Kahne, J., Middaugh, E., MacGill, A., Evans, C., & Vitak, J. (2008). *Teens, video games, and civics.* Pew Research Center: Internet and Technology. Retrieved from http://www.pewinternet.org/2008/09/16/teens-video-games-and-civics/

McGonigal, J. (2010, February). *Jane McGonigal: Gaming can make a better world* [Video file]. Retrieved from https://www.ted.com/talks/jane_mcgonigal_gaming_can_make_a_better_world

Reddit. (2016). *FFXIV gamers ages 13–20, what is your experience with FFXIV and the FFXIV gaming community.* Retrieved October 10, 2016, from https://www.reddit.com/r/ffxiv/comments/52lzzp/ffxiv_gamers_ages_1320_what_are_your_experiences

Spradley, J. P. (1980). *Participant observation.* Belmont, CA: Wadsworth.

Square Enix. (2013). *Final fantasy XIV: A realm reborn* [Video game].

Yee, N. (2009). *The Daedalus project.* Retrieved from http://www.nickyee.com/daedalus/archives/001648.php

Zichermann, G. (2011, June). *Gabe Zichermann: How games make kids smarter* [Video file]. Retrieved from https://www.ted.com/talks/gabe_zichermann_how_games_make_kids_smarter

Index

21st-century literacy   6, 39, 44, 45, 98, 107

adolescence   22, 23, 32, 34–37, 39, 47, 85, 90, 96, 97, 100, 104, 105, 107
after-school   28–30, 32
alternate reality game (ARG)   14, 17, 18
Anansi   14, 16, 18–20
Ask Anansi   14, 16, 18–20
audience   49, 55, 71–73, 77–80
augmented reality   57, 71, 76, 78
authentic   22, 30, 31, 39, 45, 48

boy culture   36, 39, 44
boys and gaming   35

civic   1, 20, 65, 67–80
classroom   1, 2, 6, 11, 14–20, 22, 29, 30, 34–36, 39, 40, 42, 43, 45, 47, 49, 54, 55, 58, 66, 68–70, 72, 73, 76, 78, 79, 98, 107
classroom practice   19, 55, 98
commercial off the shelf (COTS) games, adolescents   35, 39, 42, 43
Common Core   39, 41, 69
communication   26, 27, 37, 46, 55, 69, 71, 77, 90
communicative resource   58
community   1, 2, 6, 11, 12, 14–19, 22, 23, 25, 29–32, 35, 39, 45, 59, 67, 69, 72–75, 77–80, 97, 100–106
critical   2, 14, 16, 18, 19, 22, 23, 27, 31, 40, 42, 45, 48, 68–71, 74, 77, 78, 80, 90
critical pedagogy   19
culture   1, 3, 4, 11, 12, 16, 19, 20, 23, 26, 27, 31, 35, 36, 38–40, 43–46, 49, 53, 57, 65, 66, 70, 76, 86, 87, 93, 96, 100, 103, 105–107

development   2, 22, 24–26, 28, 31, 32, 35, 37, 39, 42, 44, 45, 47, 49, 68–70, 76, 86, 90, 92, 101
digital   1, 3, 5, 11, 12, 27, 31, 37, 40–46, 67, 71, 74, 76, 77, 80, 85, 90, 93, 98, 106
digital literacy   4, 34
diversity   23
doers   60

educational technology   42, 44, 45
educator   2, 4, 14, 32, 35, 39, 40, 41, 44, 45, 54, 59, 67, 72, 73, 75–79, 96–100, 106, 107
engagement   2, 12, 16, 19, 23–26, 35–37, 40, 45, 67–72, 74, 76, 78, 90
experiential   22, 30

fan culture   26, 105
fantasy   41, 72, 77, 85–94
final fantasy   96, 99
Final Fantasy XIV (FFXIV)   97–99, 102

game design   22, 23, 27, 29–32, 42, 55, 73, 77
game literacy   1–6, 11, 12, 14, 18, 34–39, 42–44, 47, 48, 53, 59, 60, 65–70, 72, 75, 77, 80, 88, 93, 96–98, 100, 103, 106, 107
gameplay   1, 14, 16, 18, 19, 35, 47, 100–102, 105
gamer researcher   59, 61
games   1–6, 11, 12, 14, 16, 27–29, 53, 54, 56, 58, 60, 61, 65, 71–73, 76, 79, 88, 89, 93, 96–98, 102, 106
gaming   1–6, 11, 12, 14, 16, 22, 26, 34–37, 39, 42–45, 53–57, 59, 61, 65, 72, 74, 78, 79, 96, 101, 104
Gee, James Paul   4, 6, 12, 36, 37, 45, 53–61, 88, 89, 95, 105
gender and classroom culture   107
gender and technology
genre   23–25, 32, 36, 58, 59, 65, 85, 94
geocache   74, 75, 78
geospatial   67, 68, 71–80
Global Kids Online   74
Global Positioning System (GPS)   68, 73

identity   23–25, 31, 32, 42, 86, 88, 94, 96, 97, 99
identity in games   59, 88, 89, 101, 102
implied reader   86, 87, 89–91, 94
ingress   78
integrating gaming into classes   42, 73
interest   1, 2, 12, 16, 22–26, 29–32, 34, 37, 38, 41, 44, 46, 56, 60, 68, 71–74, 90, 101, 105, 106

Jenkins, Henry   86, 93, 103, 105

learning   1, 2, 4–6, 11, 12, 14, 16, 17, 19, 20, 22–27, 30–32, 35–40, 42–48, 53, 54, 57, 58, 61, 65, 66, 68, 69, 71–73, 75, 76, 79, 107

learning sciences   40
literacy/literacies   1–6, 11, 12, 14, 18, 34–39, 42–44, 47, 48, 53, 59, 60, 65–70, 72, 75, 77, 80, 88, 93, 96–98, 100, 103, 106, 107
ludic postmodernism   55

Magic Circle   3, 16
maker education   22
makers   22, 23, 26, 27, 30–32, 42, 44, 60, 70, 106
meaning-making   36, 37, 39, 40, 44, 45
media   12, 15, 18, 19, 23–27, 30, 32, 34, 43, 47, 49, 67, 70, 71, 74, 76, 77, 79, 80, 103, 107
media literacy   80
Minecraft   65, 85, 86, 92, 93
Massively Multiplayer Online Role-Playing Game (MMORPG)   96, 98–101, 105
Multiplayer Online Battle Arena (MOBA)   57
Modders   60
Motivation   19, 22, 28, 36, 39, 45, 59, 69
multimodality   1, 61, 65, 97, 104

new media   23, 25–27, 32, 107
new media literacy   103

Out of Eden   79

paratext   86
participant observation   100
participatory
    culture   65, 66, 86, 87, 93, 96, 100, 102, 103, 105–107,
    politics   67
pedagogy   1, 6, 19, 20, 55, 93, 107
physical context   30
pixel arts game education   27, 28
playography   42
Pokemon Go   77–79,
practice   1, 3–6, 11, 14, 18, 19, 25, 28, 29, 31, 34, 36–39, 53, 55, 59, 61, 65, 67–69, 71, 75, 80, 96–98, 101, 105–107

QR codes   17

reader response   87, 88
research   2–6, 11, 12, 14–19, 22–26, 36, 39, 42, 43, 48, 53–56, 59–61, 65, 69–71, 73–75, 78, 90, 96, 100, 101
retellings   85, 90

role-playing games   88, 96–99, 102

Scavenger Hunt   17–19
school/schooling   1, 2, 14–20, 22, 23, 27–30, 32, 35–38, 40, 42–44, 53, 56, 60, 61, 68, 73, 75, 80, 85, 96, 101, 105
sociocultural research   4, 19, 23, 37, 39
South Central   14–16, 19, 20
spiders   14, 16, 17
Square Enix   98, 106
Science, Technology, Engineering, & Mathematics (STEM)   23, 29, 93
storytelling   15, 58
student inquiry   15, 16
student(s)   1, 14–20, 28, 30, 34, 35, 39–49, 54, 55, 58, 61, 68–80, 85, 94, 96, 98, 101, 107

technology   22, 23, 27, 29, 31, 32, 39, 42, 44, 55, 56, 68, 71–75, 79, 80
tech-savvy   56
text   2, 6, 37, 38, 40, 41, 46, 69–71, 74, 85–89, 93–95, 100, 102
The Inheritance Cycle   85, 86, 89, 90, 93, 95
tools   2, 5, 22, 23, 25, 27, 29–32, 35, 36, 38, 44, 46, 56, 67, 68, 71, 73, 92, 98, 107

urban education   75

verisimilitude   86, 87, 89–91, 94
video games   12, 34–40, 42–45, 47, 48, 53, 54, 58, 60, 61, 65, 71–73, 76, 79, 88, 89, 93, 96–98, 102, 106
    and adolescents   22, 23, 32, 34–37, 39, 47, 85, 90, 96, 97, 100, 104, 105, 107
video gaming   1–6, 11, 12, 14, 16, 22, 26, 34–37, 39, 42–45, 53–57, 59, 61, 65, 72, 74, 78, 79, 96, 101, 104
virtual world   1–6, 41, 65, 96, 97
world(s)   1–6, 11, 14, 19, 37, 41, 55, 57, 60, 65, 66, 71–75, 85–101, 103–106

youth   2, 6, 11, 12, 14–16, 18, 22–32, 61, 67, 68, 70, 71, 74, 75, 79, 80
Youth Participatory Action Research (YPAR)   14–16, 18, 19
youth voices   79

www.ingramcontent.com/pod-product-compliance
Lightning Source LLC
Chambersburg PA
CBHW061418300426
44114CB00015B/1983